Public Speaking

By

Clarence Stratton

CHAPTER I

SPEECH

Importance of Speech. There never has been in the history of the world a time when the spoken word has been equaled in value and importance by any other means of communication. If one traces the development of mankind from what he considers its earliest stage he will find that the wandering family of savages depended entirely upon what its members said to one another. A little later when a group of families made a clan or tribe the individuals still heard the commands of the leader, or in tribal council voiced their own opinions. The beginnings of poetry show us the bard who recited to his audiences. Drama, in all primitive societies a valuable spreader of knowledge, entertainment, and religion, is entirely oral. In so late and well-organized communities as the city republics of Greece all matters were discussed in open assemblies of the rather small populations.

Every great epoch of the world's progress shows the supreme importance of speech upon human action—individual and collective. In the Roman Forum were made speeches that affected the entire ancient world. Renaissance Italy, imperial Spain, unwieldy Russia, freedom-loving England, revolutionary France, all experienced periods when the power of certain men to speak stirred other men into tempestuous action.

The history of the United States might almost be written as the continuous record of the influence of great speakers upon others. The colonists were led to concerted action by persuasive speeches. The Colonial Congresses and Constitutional Convention were dominated by powerful orators. The history of the slavery problem is mainly the story of famous speeches and debates. Most of the active representative Americans have been leaders because of their ability to impress their fellows by their power of expressing sentiments and enthusiasms which all would voice if they could. Presidents have been nominated and candidates elected because of this equipment.

During the Great War the millions of the world were as much concerned with what some of their leaders were saying as with what their other leaders were doing.[1]

[1] See *Great American Speeches*, edited by Clarence Stratton, Lippincott and Company.

Speech in Modern Life. There is no aspect of modern life in which the spoken work is not supreme in importance. Representatives of the nations of the world deciding upon a peace treaty and deliberating upon a League of Nations sway and are swayed by speech. National assemblies—from the strangely named new ones of infant nations to the century-old organizations —speak, and listen to speeches. In state legislatures, municipal councils, law courts, religious organizations, theaters, lodges, societies, boards of directors, stockholders' meetings, business discussions, classrooms, dinner parties, social functions, friendly calls—in every human relationship where two people meet there is communication by means of speech.

Scientific invention keeps moving as rapidly as it can to take advantage of this supreme importance. Great as was the advance marked by the telegraph, it was soon overtaken and passed by the convenience of the telephone. The first conveys messages at great distance, but it fails to give the answer at once. It fails to provide for the rapid *interchange* of ideas which the second affords. Wireless telegraphy has already been followed by wireless telephony. The rapid intelligent disposal of the complicated affairs of our modern world requires more than mere writing—it demands immediate interchange of ideas by means of speech.

Many people who in their habitual occupations are popularly said to write a great deal do nothing of the sort. The millions of typists in the world do no writing at all in the real sense of that word; they merely reproduce what some one else has actually composed and dictated. This latter person also does no actual writing. He speaks what he wants to have put into writing. Dictating is not an easily acquired accomplishment in business—as many a man will testify. Modern office practice has intensified the difficulty. It may be rather disconcerting to deliver well-constructed, meaningful sentences to an unresponsive stenographer, but at any rate the receiver is alive. But to talk into the metallic receiver of a mechanical dictaphone has an almost ridiculous air. Men have to train themselves deliberately to speak well when they first begin to use these time-saving devices. Outside of business, a great deal of the material printed in periodicals and books—sometimes long novels—has been delivered orally, and not written at all by its author. Were anything more needed to show how much speech is used it would be furnished by the reports of the telephone companies. In one table the number of daily connections in 1895 was 2,351,420. In 1918 this item had increased to 31,263,611. In twenty-three years the calls had grown fifteen times as numerous. In 1882 there were 100,000 subscriber stations. In 1918 this number had swelled to 11,000,000.

Subordinates and executives in all forms of business could save incalculable time and annoyance by being able to present their material clearly and forcefully over the telephone, as well as in direct face-to-face intercourse.

The Director of high schools in a large municipality addressed a circular letter to the business firms of the city, asking them to state what is most necessary in order to fit boys for success in business. Ninety-nine per cent laid stress on the advantage of being able to write and speak English accurately and forcibly.

Testimony in support of the statement that training in speaking is of paramount importance in all careers might be adduced from a score of sources. Even from the seemingly far-removed phase of military leadership comes the same support. The following paragraph is part of a letter issued by the office of the Adjutant-General during the early months of the participation of this country in the Great War.

> "A great number of men have failed at camp because of inability to articulate clearly. A man who cannot impart his idea to his command in clear distinct language, and with sufficient volume of voice to be heard reasonably far, is not qualified to give command upon which human life will depend. Many men disqualified by this handicap might have become officers under their country's flag had they been properly trained in school and college. It is to be hoped therefore that more emphasis will be placed upon the basic principles of elocution in the training of

our youth. Even without prescribed training in elocution a great improvement could be wrought by the instructors in our schools and colleges, regardless of the subjects, by insisting that all answers be given in a loud, clear, well rounded voice which, of course, necessitates the opening of the mouth and free movement of the lips. It is remarkable how many excellent men suffer from this handicap, and how almost impossible it is to correct this after the formative years of life."

Perhaps the most concise summary of the relative values of exercise in the three different forms of communication through language was enunciated by Francis Bacon in his essay entitled *Studies*, published first in 1597: "Reading maketh a full man; conference a ready man; and writing an exact man."

Speech and Talk. The high value here placed upon speech must not be transferred to mere talk. The babbler will always be justly regarded with contempt. Without ideas, opinions, information, talk becomes the most wasteful product in the world, wasteful not only of the time of the person who insists upon delivering it, but more woefully and unjustifiably wasteful of the time and patience of those poor victims who are forced to listen to it. Shakespeare put a man of this disposition into *The Merchant of Venice* and then had his discourse described by another.

> "Gratiano speaks an infinite deal of nothing, more than any man in all Venice. His reasons are as two grains of wheat hid in two bushels of chaff: you shall seek all day 'ere you find them, and when you have them, they are not worth the search."

But the man who has ideas and can best express them is a leader everywhere. He does the organizing, he makes and imparts the plans, he carries his own theories and beliefs into execution, he is the intrusted agent, the advanced executive. He can act for himself. He can influence others to significant and purposeful action. The advantages that come to men who can think upon their feet, who can express extempore a carefully considered proposition, who can adapt their conversation or arguments to every changing condition, cannot be emphasized too strongly.

Speech an Acquired Ability. We frequently regard and discuss speech as a perfectly natural attribute of all human beings. In some sense it is. Yet an American child left to the care of deaf-mutes, never hearing the speech of his own kind, would not develop into a speaker of the native language of his parents. He doubtless would be able to imitate every natural sound he might hear. He could reproduce the cry or utterance of every animal or bird he had ever heard. But he would no more speak English naturally than he would Arabic. In this sense, language is not a natural attribute as is hunger. It is an imitative accomplishment acquired only after long years of patient practice and arduous effort. Some people never really attain a facile mastery of the means of communication. Some mature men and women are no more advanced in the use of speech than children of ten or fifteen. The practice is life-long. The effort is unceasing.

A child seems to be as well adapted to learning one language as another. There may be certain physical formations or powers inherited from a race which predispose the easier mastery of a language, but even these handicaps for learning a different tongue can be overcome by imitation, study, and practice. Any child can be taught an alien tongue through constant companionship of nurse or governess. The second generation of immigrants to this country learns our speech even while it may continue the tongue of the native land. The third generation—if it mix continuously with speakers of English—relinquishes entirely the exercise of the mother tongue. The succeeding generation seldom can speak it, frequently cannot even understand it.

Training to Acquire Speech Ability. The methods by which older persons may improve their ability to speak are analogous to those just suggested as operative for children, except that the more mature the person the wider is his range of models to imitate, of examples from which to make deductions; the more resources he has within himself and about him for self-development and improvement. A child's vocabulary increases rapidly through new experiences. A mature person can create new surroundings. He can deliberately widen his horizon either by reading or association. The child is mentally alert. A man can keep himself intellectually alert. A child delights in his use of his powers of expression. A man can easily make his intercourse a source of delight to himself and to all with whom he comes in contact. A child's imagination is kept stimulated continually. A man can consciously stimulate either his imagination or his reason. In the democracy of childhood the ability to impress companions depends to a great extent upon the ability to speak. There is no necessity of following the parallel any farther.

Good speakers, then, are made, not born. Training counts for as much as natural ability. In fact if a person considers carefully the careers of men whose ability to speak has impressed the world by its preeminence he will incline to the conclusion that the majority of them were not to any signal extent born speakers at all. In nearly all cases of great speakers who have left records of their own progress in this powerful art their testimony is that without the effort to improve, without the unceasing practice they would have always remained no more marked for this so-called gift than all others.

Overcoming Drawbacks. According to the regularly repeated tradition the great Greek orator, Demosthenes, overcame impediments that would have daunted any ordinary man. His voice was weak. He lisped, and his manner was awkward. With pebbles in his mouth he tried his lungs against the noise of the dashing waves. This strengthened his voice and gave him presence of mind in case of tumult among his listeners. He declaimed as he ran uphill. Whether these traditions be true or not, their basis must be that it was only by rigorous training that he did become a tolerable speaker. The significant point, however, is that with apparent handicaps he did develop his ability until he became great.

Charles James Fox began his parliamentary career by being decidedly awkward and filling his speeches with needless repetitions, yet he became renowned as one of Great Britain's most brilliant speakers and statesmen.

Henry Clay clearly describes his own exercises in self-training when he was quite a grown man.

> "I owe my success in life to one single fact, namely, at the age of twenty-seven I commenced, and continued for years, the practice of daily reading and speaking upon the contents of some historical or scientific book. These offhand efforts were made sometimes in a corn field, at others in the forests, and not infrequently in some distant barn with the horse and ox for my auditors. It is to this early practice in the art of all arts that I am

indebted to the primary and leading impulses that stimulated me forward, and shaped and molded my entire destiny."

Abraham Lincoln never let pass any opportunity to try to make a speech. His early employers, when called upon after his fame was won to describe his habits as a young man, admitted that they might have been disposed to consider him an idle fellow. They explained that he was not only idle himself but the cause of idleness in others. Unless closely watched, he was likely to mount a stump and, to the intense delight of his fellow farm hands, deliver a side-splitting imitation of some itinerant preacher or a stirring political harangue.

The American whose reputation for speech is the greatest won it more through training than by natural gift.

> "I could not speak before the school," said Daniel Webster. ... "Many a piece did I commit to memory and rehearse in my room over and over again, but when the day came, and the schoolmaster called my name, and I saw all eyes turned upon my seat, I could not raise myself from it.... Mr. Buckminster always pressed and entreated, most winningly, that I would venture, but I could never command sufficient resolution. When the occasion was over I went home and wept bitter tears of mortification."

Results of Training. The significance of all these illustrations is that no great speaker has come by his ability without careful and persistent training. No molder of the world's destinies springs fully equipped from the welter of promiscuous events. He has been training for a long time. On the other hand the much more practical lesson to be derived from these biographical excerpts is that these men started from ordinary conditions to make themselves into forceful thinkers with powers of convincing expression. They overcame handicaps. They strengthened their voices. They learned how to prepare and arrange material. They made themselves able to explain topics to others. They knew so well the reasons for their own belief that they could convince others.

In a smaller way, to a lesser degree, any person can do the same thing, and by the same or similar methods. Barring some people who have physical defects or nervous diseases, any person who has enough brains to grasp an idea, to form an opinion, or to produce a thought, can be made to speak well. The preceding sentence says "barring some people who have physical defects" because not all so handicapped at the beginning need despair of learning to improve in speaking ability. By systems in which the results appear almost miraculous the dumb are now taught to speak. Stutterers and stammerers become excellent deliverers of speeches in public. Weak voices are strengthened. Hesitant expressions are made coherent. Such marvels of modern science belong, however, to special classes and institutions. They are cited here to prove that in language training today practically nothing is impossible to the teacher with knowledge and patience in educating students with alertness and persistence.

Practical Help. This book attempts to provide a guide for such teachers and students. It aims to be eminently practical. It is intended to help students to improve in speech. It assumes that those who use it are able to speak their language with some facility—at least they can pronounce its usual words. That and the realization that one is alive, as indicated by a mental openness to ideas and an intellectual alertness about most things in the universe, are all that are absolutely required of a beginner who tries to improve in speaking. Practically all else can be added unto him.

As this volume has a definite aim it has a simple practical basis. It will not soar too far above the essentials. It tries not to offer an elaborate explanation of an enthymeme when the embryonic speaker's knees are knocking together so loudly that he can not hear the instructor's correcting pronunciation of the name. It takes into account that when a beginner stands before an audience—and this is true not only the first time—even his body is not under his control. Lips grow cold and dry; perspiration gushes from every pore of the brow and runs down the face; legs grow weak; eyes see nothing; hands swell to enormous proportions; violent pains shoot across the chest; the breath is confined within the lungs; from the clapper-like tongue comes only a faint click. Is it any wonder that under such physical agonies the mind refuses to respond—rather, is incapable of any action whatever?

Speech Based on Thought and Language. Every speech is a result of the combination of thought and language, of material and expression. It would be quite possible to begin with considerations of the thought content of speeches—the material; but this book begins with the other;—the language, the expression. If this order have no other advantage, it does possess this one;—that during the informal discussions and expressions of opinion occasioned by the early chapters and exercises, members of the class are attaining a feeling of ease in speaking among themselves which will later eradicate a great deal of the nervousness usually experienced when speaking *before* the class. In addition, some attention to such topics as voice, tone, pronunciation, common errors, use of the dictionary, vocabulary, may instil habits of self-criticism and observation which may save from doubt and embarrassing mistakes later.

EXERCISES

1. Recall some recent speech you heard. In parallel columns make lists of its excellences and deficiencies.

2. Give the class an account of the occasion, the purpose of the speaker, and his effect upon his audience, or upon you.

3. Explain how children learn to speak.

4. From your observation give the class an account of how young children enlarge their vocabularies.

5. Using the material of this chapter as the basis of your remarks, show the value of public speaking.

6. Of what value is public speaking to women?

7. What effects upon speeches by women will universal suffrage have?

8. Choose some profession—as law, engineering—and show how an ability to speak may be of value in it.

9. Choose some business position, and show how an ability to speak is a decided advantage in it.

10. What is the best method of acquiring a foreign language? For example, how shall the alien learn English?

11. Choose some great man whom you admire. Show how he became a speaker. Or give an account of one of his speeches.

12. Show the value of public speaking to a girl—in school; in business; in other careers.

13. Explain the operation of a dictaphone.

14. How can training in public speaking help an applicant for a position?

15. Explain the sentence quoted from Bacon's essay on studies.

CHAPTER II

THE VOICE

Organs of Speech. Although the effects produced by the human voice are myriad in their complexity, the apparatus involved in making the sounds which constitute speech is extremely simple. In construction it has been usually compared to an organ pipe, a comparison justifiable for imparting a non-technical understanding of its operation.

An organ pipe is a tube in which a current of air passing over the edge of a piece of metal causes it to vibrate, thus putting into motion the column of air in the pipe which then produces a note. The operating air is forced across the sounding piece of metal from a bellows. The tube in which the thin sounding plate and the column of air vibrate acts as a resonator. The resulting sound depends upon various sizes of the producing parts. If the tube is quite long the sound is low in pitch. If the tube is short the sound is high. Stopping the end of the pipe or leaving it open alters the pitch. A stopped pipe gives a note an octave lower than an open pipe of the same length. The amount of the vibrating plate which is allowed to move also determines the pitch of a note. If the air is under great pressure the note is loud. If the air is under little pressure the note is soft.

It is quite easy to transfer this explanation to the voice-producing apparatus in the human body.

To the bellows correspond the lungs from which the expelled air is forced upwards through the windpipe. The lungs are able to expel air regularly and gently, with no more expense of energy than ordinary breathing requires. But the lungs can also force air out with tremendous power—power enough to carry sound over hundreds of yards. In ordinary repose the outward moving breath produces no sound whatever, for it meets in its passage no obstruction.

Producing Tone. At the upper end of the windpipe is a triangular chamber, the front angle of which forms the Adam's apple. In this are the vocal cords.

These cords are two tapes of membrane which can be brought closely together, and by muscular tension stretched until passing air causes them to vibrate. They in turn cause the air above them to vibrate, much as the air in an organ pipe vibrates. Thus tone is produced.

The air above the vocal cords may fill all the open spaces above the larynx —the throat, the mouth, the nasal cavity in the head, the nostrils. This rather large amount of air, vibrating freely, produces a sound low in pitch. The larger the cavities are made the lower the pitch. You can verify this by producing a note. Then place your finger upon your Adam's apple. Produce a sound lower in pitch. Notice what your larynx does. Sing a few notes down the scale or up to observe the same principle of the change of pitch in the human voice.

Producing Vowels. If the mouth be kept wide open and no other organ be allowed to modify or interrupt the sound a vowel is produced. In speech every part of the head that can be used is brought into action to modify these uninterrupted vibrations of vocal cords and air. The lips, the cheeks, the teeth, the tongue, the hard palate, the soft palate, the nasal cavity, all coöperate to make articulate speech.

As in its mechanism, so in the essence of its modifications, the human voice is a marvel of simplicity. If the mouth be opened naturally and the tongue and lips be kept as much out of the way as in ordinary breathing, and then the vocal cords be made to vibrate, the resulting sound will be the vowel *a* as in *father*. If now, starting from that same position and with that same vowel sound, the tongue be gradually raised the sound will be modified. Try it. The sound will pass through other vowels. Near the middle position it will sound like *a* in *fate*; and when the tongue gets quite close to the roof of the mouth without touching it the vowel will be the *e* of *feet*. Others—such as the *i* of *it*—can be distinguished clearly.

Starting again from that same open position and with that same vowel sound, *ah,* if the tongue be allowed to lie flat, but the lips be gradually closed and at the same time rounded, the sound will pass from *ah* to the *o* of *hope,* then on to the *oo* of *troop*. The *oa* of *broad* and other vowels can be distinguished at various positions.

By moving lips and tongue at the same time an almost infinite variety of vowel sounds can be made.

Producing Consonants. In order to produce consonant sounds the other parts of the speaking apparatus are brought into operation. Everyone of them has some function in the formation of some consonant by interrupting or checking the breath. A student, by observing or feeling the motions of his mouth can easily instruct himself in the importance of each part if he will carefully pronounce a few times all the various consonant sounds of the language.

The lips produce the sounds of *p*, *b*, *wh*, and *w*. The lips and teeth produce the sounds of *f*, *v*. The tongue and teeth together make the sounds of *th* and *dh*. The tongue in conjunction with the forward portion of the hard palate produces several sounds—*t*, *d*, *s*, *z*, *r*, and *l*. The tongue operating against or near the rear of the hard palate pronounces *ch*, *j*, *sh*, *zh*, and a different *r*. To make the consonant *y* the tongue, the hard palate, and the soft palate operate. The tongue and soft palate make *k* and *g*. A strong breathing makes the sound of *h*. By including the nasal passages in conjunction with some of the other parts here listed the so-called nasals, *m*, *n*, and *ng*, are made. According to the organ involved our consonant sounds are conveniently grouped as labials (lips), dentals (teeth), linguals (tongue), palatals (palate), and nasals (nose).

The correct position and action of the vocal organs are of supreme importance to all speakers. Many an inveterate stammerer, stutterer, or repeater can be relieved, if not cured, of the embarrassing impediment by attention to the position of his speech organs and by careful, persistent practice in their manipulation. In fact every speaker must be cognizant of the placement of these parts if he desires to have control over his speech. Frequently it is such correct placement rather than loud noise or force which carries expressions clearly to listeners.

While it is true that singing will strengthen the lungs and help in control of breath, it is not always the fact—as might be expected—that singing will develop the speaking voice. Not every person who can sing has a pleasant or forceful voice in ordinary discourse. In singing, to secure purity of musical tone, the vowels are likely to be disproportionately dwelt upon.

Thus we have the endless *la-la-la* and *ah-ah* of so many vocal show-pieces. The same practice leads to the repeated criticism that it makes no difference whether a song be in English or a foreign language—the listeners understand just as much in either case.

In speaking effectively the aim and method are the exact opposite. When a man speaks he wants to be listened to for the meaning of what he is uttering. There are so many words in the language with the same or similar vowel sounds that only the sharpest discrimination by means of consonants permits of their being intelligible. The speaker, therefore, will exercise the greatest care in pronouncing consonants distinctly. As these sounds usually begin and end words, and as they are produced by rather sudden checks or interruptions, they can be made to produce a wave motion in the air which will carry the entire word safely and clearly beyond the ear into the understanding. In public speaking no amount of care and attention bestowed upon pronouncing consonants can be spared.

Tone. The most marked quality of a person's voice is its tone. It will be enough for the purposes of this manual to assert that the tone should be both clear and agreeable. In public speaking the first of these is all important, though an absence of the second qualification may almost neutralize all the advantages of the first. Clearness may be impaired by several causes. The speaker may feel that his throat closes up, that he becomes choked. His tongue may become stiff and "cleave to the roof of his mouth"—as the feeling is popularly described. He may breathe so energetically that the escaping or entering air makes more noise than the words themselves. He may be more or less conscious of all these. The others he may not discover for himself. The instructor or members of the class will inform him of their presence. Set jaws will prevent him from opening his mouth wide enough and operating his lips flexibly enough to speak with a full tone. A nasal quality results mainly from lack of free resonance in the head and nose passages. Adenoids and colds in the head produce this condition. It should be eradicated by advice and practice.

Usually whatever corrections will make the tone clearer will also make it more agreeable. The nasal pessimistic whine is not a pleasant recommendation of personality. High, forced, strident tones produce not only irritation in the listener but throat trouble for the speaker.

Articulate—that is, connected—speech may be considered with reference to four elements, all of which are constantly present in any spoken discourse.

Speed. First, there is the speed of delivery. An angry woman can utter more words in a minute than any one wants to hear. The general principle underlying all speech delivery is that as the audience increases in number the rapidity of utterance should be lessened. Those who are accustomed to addressing large audiences, or to speaking in the open air, speak very slowly. A second consideration is the material being delivered. Easily grasped narrative, description, and explanation, simply phrased and directly constructed, may be delivered much more rapidly than involved explanation, unfamiliar phraseology, long and intricate sentence constructions, unusual material, abstract reasoning, and unwelcome sentiments. The beginnings of speeches move much more slowly than later parts. A speaker who intends to lead an audience a long distance, or to hold the attention for a long time, will be extremely careful not to speak at the beginning so rapidly that he leaves them far behind.

This does not mean that a speaker must drawl his words. One of our national characteristics is that we shorten our words in pronouncing them— *ing* generally loses the *g, does not* has become *doesn't* and quite incorrectly *don't, yes* is *yeeh,* etc. In many cases nothing more is required than the restoration of the word to its correct form. Some words can easily be lengthened because of the significance of their meanings. Others must be extended in order to carry. The best method of keeping down the rate of delivery is by a judicious use of pauses. Pauses are to the listener what punctuation marks are to the reader. He is not conscious of their presence, but he would be left floundering if they were absent. Some of the most effective parts of speeches are the pauses. They impart clearness to ideas, as well as aiding in emphasis and rhythm.

Pitch. A second quality of speech is its pitch. This simply means its place in the musical scale. Speaking voices are high, medium, or low. Unfortunate tendencies of Americans seem to be for women to pitch their voices too high, with resultant strain and unpleasantness, and for men to pitch their voices too low, with resultant growls and gruffness. The voices of young children should be carefully guarded in this respect; so should the changing voices of growing boys. To secure a good pitch for the speaking voice the normal natural pitch of usual conversation should be found. Speech in that same pitch should be developed for larger audiences. Frequently a better pitch can be secured by slightly lowering the voice. If the natural pitch be too low for clearness or agreeableness it should be slightly raised—never more than is absolutely necessary.

No connected group of words should be delivered in a monotonously level pitch. The voice must rise and fall. These changes must answer intelligently to the meaning of the material. Such variations are called inflections. The most disagreeable violations of required inflections are raising the voice where it should fall—as at the completion of an idea, and letting it drop where it should remain up—as before the completion of an idea, frequently answering to a comma. Other variations of pitch depend upon emphasis.

Emphasis. Emphasis is giving prominence to a word or phrase so that its importance is impressed upon a listener. This result is most easily secured by contrast. More force may be put into its delivery than the rest of the speech. The word may be made louder or not so loud. The voice may be pitched higher or lower. The word may be lengthened. Pauses will make it prominent. In speaking, combinations of these are employed to produce emphasis.

While all qualities of speech are important, emphasis is of cardinal value. Listeners will never recall everything that a speaker has said. By a skilful employment of emphasis he will put into their consciousness the main theme of his message, the salient arguments of his contention, the leading motives of action. Here again is that close interdependence of manner and material referred to in the preceding chapter. In later chapters will be discussed various methods of determining and securing emphasis of larger sections than mere words and phrases.

Phrasing. Somewhat related to emphasis is phrasing. This is the grouping together of words, phrases, clauses, and other units so that their meaning and significance may be easily grasped by a listener. As has been already said, pauses serve as punctuation marks for the hearer. Short pauses correspond to commas, longer ones to colons and semi-colons, marked ones to periods. Speakers can by pauses clearly indicate the conclusions of sections, the completion of topics, the passage from one part of the material to another, the transfer of attention from one subject to its opposite. Within smaller range pauses can add delightful variety to delivery as they can signally reinforce the interpretation. No speaker should fall into the habit of monotonously letting his pauses mark the limit of his breath capacity, nor should he take any regular phrase, clause, or sentence length to be indicated by pauses. In this as in all other aspects variety is the charm of speech.

Enunciation. No matter what handicaps a person may have he may overcome them to secure a distinct, agreeable enunciation. Care in enunciating words will enable a speaker to be heard almost anywhere. It is recorded that John Fox, a famous preacher of South Place Chapel, London, whose voice was neither loud nor strong, was heard in every part of Covent Garden Theatre, seating 3500, when he made anti-corn-law orations, by the clearness with which he pronounced the final consonants of the words he spoke.

One of the orators best known to readers is Edmund Burke, whose speeches are studied as models of argumentative arrangement and style. Yet in actual speech-making Burke was more or less a failure because of the unfortunate method of his delivery. Many men markedly inferior in capacity to Burke overcame disadvantageous accidents, but he was frequently hurried and impetuous. Though his tones were naturally sonorous, they were harsh; and he never divested his speech of a strong Irish accent. Then, too, his gestures were clumsy. These facts will explain to us who read and study leisurely these masterpieces why they failed of their purpose when presented by their gifted but ineffective author.

Pronunciation. Enunciation depends to a great degree upon pronunciation. The pronunciation of a word is no fixed and unchangeable thing. Every district of a land may have its peculiar local sounds, every succeeding generation may vary the manner of accenting a word. English people today pronounce *schedule* with a soft *ch* sound. *Program* has had its accent shifted from the last to the first syllable. Many words have two regularly heard pronunciations—*neither, advertisement, Elizabethan, rations, oblique, route, quinine,* etc. Fashions come and go in pronunciation as in all other human interests. Some sounds stamp themselves as carelessnesses or perversions at once and are never admitted into educated, cultured speech. Others thrive and have their day, only to fade before some more widely accepted pronunciation. The first rule in pronunciation is to consult a good dictionary. This will help in most cases but not in all, for a dictionary merely records all accepted sounds; only partly can it point out the better of disputed sounds by placing it first. Secondly, speech is a living, growing, changing thing. Dictionaries drop behind the times surprisingly rapidly. The regularly accepted sound may have come into general use after the dictionary was printed. New activities, unusual phases of life may throw into general conversation thousands of unused, unheard words. This was true of the recent Great War, when with little or no preparation thousands of military, industrial, naval, and aeronautical terms came into daily use. Discussions still flutter mildly around *cantonment* and *rations*, and a score of others.

Next to authoritative books, the best models are to be secured from the speech of authorities in each branch to which the term specifically belongs. Thus the military leaders have made the pronunciation of *oblique* with the long *i* the correct one for all military usages. The accepted sound of *cantonments* was fixed by the men who built and controlled them. As it is not always possible for the ordinary person to hear such authorities deliver such terms in discourse one can merely say that a familiarity with correct pronunciation can be secured only like liberty—at the price of eternal vigilance.

Constant consultation of the dictionary and other books of recognized reference value, close observance of the speech of others, scrutiny of one's own pronunciation, mental criticism of others' slips, and determination to correct one's own errors, are the various methods of attaining certainty of correct delivery of word sounds.

Poise. When a speaker stands before an audience to address its members he should be perfectly at ease. Physical ease will produce an effect upon the listeners. Mental ease because of mastery of the material will induce confidence in the delivery. Bodily eccentricities and awkwardness which detract from the speech itself should be eradicated by strenuous practice. Pose and poise should first command respectful attention. The body should be erect, but not stiff. Most of the muscles should be relaxed. The feet should be naturally placed, not so far apart as to suggest straddling, not so close together as to suggest the military stand at "attention."

What should be done with the hands? Nothing. They should not be clasped; they should not be put behind the back; they should not be jammed into pockets; the arms should not be held akimbo; they should not be folded. Merely let the arms and hands hang at the sides naturally.

Gestures. Should a speaker make gestures? Certainly never if the gesture detracts from the force of an expression, as when a preacher pounds the book so hard that the congregation cannot hear his words. Certainly yes, when the feeling of the speaker behind the phrase makes him enforce his meaning by a suitable movement. In speaking today fewer gestures are indulged in than years ago. There should never be many. Senseless, jerky, agitated pokings and twitchings should be eradicated completely. Insincere flourishes should be inhibited. Beginners should beware of gestures until they become such practised masters of their minds and bodies that physical emphasis may be added to spoken force.

A speaker should feel perfectly free to change his position or move his feet during his remarks. Usually such a change should be made to correspond with a pause in delivery. In this way it reinforces the indication of progress or change of topic, already cited in discussing pauses.

Delivery. A speaker should never begin to talk the very instant he has taken his place before his audience. He should make a slight pause to collect the attention before he utters his salutation (to be considered later) and should make another short pause between it and the opening sentences of his speech proper. After he has spoken the last word he should not fling away from his station to his seat. This always spoils the effect of an entire address by ruining the impression that the last phrase might have made.

As for the speech itself, there are five ways of delivering it:

1. To write it out in full and read it.

2. To write it out in full and commit it to memory.

3. To write out and memorize the opening and closing sentences and other especially important parts, leaving the rest for extempore delivery.

4. To use an outline or a brief which suggests the headings in logical order.

5. To speak without manuscript or notes.

Reading the Speech. The first of these methods—to read the speech from a prepared manuscript—really changes the speech to a lecture or reading. True, it prevents the author from saying anything he would not say in careful consideration of his topic. It assures him of getting in all he wants to say. It gives the impression that all his utterances are the result of calm, collected thinking. On the other hand, so few people can read from a manuscript convincingly that the reproduction is likely to be a dull, lifeless proceeding in which almost anything might be said, so little does the material impress the audience. This method can hardly be considered speech-making at all.

Memorizing the Speech. The second method—of repeating memorized compositions—is better. It at least seems alive. It has an appearance of direct address. It possesses the other advantages of the first method—definite reasoning and careful construction. But its dangers are grave. Few people can recite memorized passages with the personal appeal and direct significance that effective spoken discourse should have. Emphasis is lacking. Variety is absent. The tone becomes monotonous. The speech is so well committed that it flows too easily. If several speakers follow various methods, almost any listener can unerringly pick the memorized efforts. Let the speaker in delivery strive for variety, pauses, emphasis; let him be actor enough to simulate the feeling of spontaneous composition as he talks, yet no matter how successful he may be in his attempts there will still be slight inconsistencies, trifling incongruities, which will disturb a listener even if he cannot describe his mental reaction. The secret lies in the fact that written and spoken composition differ in certain details which are present in each form in spite of the utmost care to weed them out.

Memorizing Parts. The third manner can be made effective if the speaker can make the gap just described between written and spoken discourse extremely narrow. If not, his speech will appear just what it is—an incongruous patchwork of carefully prepared, reconsidered writing, and more or less spontaneously evolved speaking.

Speaking from Outline or Brief. The fourth method is by far the best for students training themselves to become public speakers. After a time the brief or outline can be retained in the mind, and the speaker passes from this method to the next. A brief for an important law case in the United States Supreme Court is a long and elaborate instrument. But a student speaker's brief or outline need not be long.

Directions, models, and exercises for constructing and using outlines will be given in a later chapter.

The Best Method. The last method is unquestionably the best. Let a man so command all the aspects of a subject that he fears no breakdown in his thoughts, let him be able to use language so that he need never hesitate for the best expression, let him know the effect he wants to make upon his audience, the time he has to do it in, and he will know by what approaches he can best reach his important theme, what he may safely omit, what he must include, what he may hurry over, what he must slowly unfold, what he may handle lightly, what he must treat seriously; in short, he will make a great speech. This manner is the ideal towards which all students, all speakers, should strive.

Attributes of the Speaker. Attributes of the speaker himself will aid or mar his speech. Among those which help are sincerity, earnestness, simplicity, fairness, self-control, sense of humor, sympathy. All great speakers have possessed these traits. Reports upon significant speakers describing their manner emphasize them. John Bright, the famous English parliamentarian of the middle of the last century, is described as follows:

His style of speaking was exactly what a conventional demagogue's ought not to be. It was pure to austerity; it was stripped of all superfluous ornament. It never gushed or foamed. It never allowed itself to be mastered by passion. The first peculiarity that struck the listener was its superb self-restraint. The orator at his most powerful passages appeared as if he were rather keeping in his strength than taxing it with effort.

JUSTIN McCARTHY: *History of Our Own Time*

In American history the greatest speeches were made by Abraham Lincoln. In Cooper Union, New York, he made in 1860 the most powerful speech against the slave power. The *New York Tribune* the next day printed this description of his manner.

> Mr. Lincoln is one of nature's orators, using his rare powers solely to elucidate and convince, though their inevitable effect is to delight and electrify as well. We present herewith a very full and accurate report of this speech; yet the tones, the gestures, the kindling eye, and the mirth-provoking look defy the reporter's skill. The vast assemblage frequently rang with cheers and shouts of applause, which were prolonged and intensified at the close. No man ever before made such an impression on his first appeal to a New York audience.

Shakespeare's Advice. Some of the best advice for speakers was written by Shakespeare as long ago as just after 1600, and although it was intended primarily for actors, its precepts are just as applicable to almost any kind of delivered discourse. Every sentence of it is full of significance for a student of speaking. Hamlet, Prince of Denmark, is airing his opinions about the proper manner of speaking upon the stage.

HAMLET'S SPEECH

Speak the speech, I pray you, as I pronounced it to you, trippingly on the tongue; but if you mouth it, as many of your players do, I had as lief the town-crier spoke my lines. Nor do not saw the air too much with your hand, thus, but use all gently; for in the very torrent, tempest, and, as I may say, whirlwind of your passion, you must acquire and beget a temperance that may give it smoothness. Oh, it offends me to the soul to hear a robustious periwig-pated fellow tear a passion to tatters, to very rags, to split the ears of the groundlings, who for the most part are capable of nothing but inexplicable dumb-shows and noise. I would have such a fellow whipped for o'erdoing Termagant. It out-herods Herod. Pray you, avoid it.

Be not too tame neither, but let your own discretion be your tutor. Suit the action to the word, the word to the action; with this special observance, that you o'erstep not the modesty of nature. For anything so overdone is from the purpose of playing, whose end, both at the first and now, was and is, to hold, as 't were, the mirror up to nature; to show virtue her own feature, scorn her own image, and the very age and body of the time his form and pressure. Now this overdone, or come tardy off, though it make the unskilful laugh, cannot but make the judicious grieve; the censure of the which one must in your allowance o'erweigh a whole theater of others. Oh, there be players that I have seen play, and heard others praise, and that highly, not to speak it profanely, that, neither having the accent of Christians nor the gait of Christian, pagan, nor man, have so strutted and bellowed that I have thought some of nature's journeymen had made men and not made them well, they imitated humanity so abominably.

Oh, reform it altogether. And let those that play your clowns speak no more than is set down for them; for there be of them that will themselves laugh, to set on some quantity of barren spectators to laugh too, though in the meantime some necessary question of the play be then to be considered. That's villainous, and shows a most pitiful ambition in the fool that uses it. Go make you ready.

EXERCISES

1. 'Neath our feet broke the brittle bright stubble like chaff.

2. The first sip of love is pleasant; the second, perilous; the third, pestilent.

3. Our ardors are ordered by our enthusiasms.

4. She's positively sick of seeing her soiled, silk, Sunday dress.

5. The rough cough and hiccough plowed me through.

6. She stood at the gate welcoming him in.

7. Five miles meandering with a mazy motion.

8. Peter Piper picked a peck of pickled peppers: if Peter Piper picked a peck of pickled peppers, where is the peck of pickled peppers that Peter Piper picked?

9. Theophilus Thistle, the thistle-sifter, sifted a sieve of unsifted thistles. If Theophilus Thistle, the thistle-sifter, sifted a sieve of unsifted thistles, where is the sieve of unsifted thistles that Theophilus Thistle, the thistle-sifter, sifted?

10.   Alone, alone, all, all alone,
            Alone on a wide, wide sea!

11.   The splendor falls on castle walls,
            And snowy summits old in story.

12.   Tomorrow and tomorrow and tomorrow
         Creeps in this petty pace from day to day
         To the last syllable of recorded time.

13.   The moan of doves in immemorial elms,
          And murmurings of innumerable bees.

14. The Ladies' Aid ladies were talking about a conversation they had overheard, before the meeting, between a man and his wife.

"They must have been at the Zoo," said Mrs. A.; "because I heard her mention 'a trained deer.'"

"Goodness me!" laughed Mrs. B. "What queer hearing you must have! They were talking about going away, and she said, 'Find out about the train, dear.'"

"Well, did anybody ever!" exclaimed Mrs. C. "I am sure they were talking about musicians, for she said, 'a trained ear,' as distinctly as could be."

The discussion began to warm up, and in the midst of it the lady herself appeared. They carried the case to her promptly, and asked for a settlement.

"Well, well, you do beat all!" she exclaimed, after hearing each one. "I'd been out in the country overnight and was asking my husband if it rained here last night."

15.

> Learning condemns beyond the reach of hope
> The careless lips that speak of sŏap for soap;
> Her edict exiles from her fair abode
> The clownish voice that utters rŏad for road;
> Less stern to him who calls his coat a cŏat,
> And steers his boat believing it a bŏat.
> She pardoned one, our classic city's boast,
> Who said at Cambridge, mŏst instead of most,
> But knit her brows and stamped her angry foot
> To hear a Teacher call a root a rŏot.

16.

> Hear the tolling of the bells—
>   Iron bells!
> What a world of solemn thought their monody compels!
>   In the silence of the night,
>   How we shiver with affright
> At the melancholy menace of their tone!
>   For every sound that floats
>   From the rust within their throats
>   Is a groan.
>   And the people—ah, the people—
>   They that dwell up in the steeple,
>   All alone,
>   And who, tolling, tolling, tolling,
>   In that muffled monotone,

                    Feel a glory in so rolling
                        On the human heart a stone—
They are neither man nor woman—
They are neither brute nor human—
                        They are Ghouls:
                    And their king it is who tolls;
                    And he rolls, rolls, rolls,
                        Rolls
                    A Paean from the bells!
                    And his merry bosom swells
                    With the paean of the bells!
                    And he dances, and he yells;
                    Keeping time, time, time,
                    In a sort of Runic rhyme,
                    To the paean of the bells—
                        Of the bells.

17.

Collecting, projecting,
Receding and speeding,
And shocking and rocking,
And darting and parting.
And threading and spreading,
And whizzing and hissing,
And dripping and skipping,
And hitting and splitting,
And shining and twining,
And rattling and battling,
And shaking and quaking,
And pouring and roaring,
And waving and raving,
And tossing and crossing,
And flowing and going,
And running and stunning,
And foaming and roaming,
And dinning and spinning,

And dropping and hopping,
And working and jerking,
And guggling and struggling,
And heaving and cleaving,
And moaning and groaning;

And glittering and frittering,
And gathering and feathering,
And whitening and brightening,
And quivering and shivering,
And hurrying and skurrying,
And thundering and floundering;

Dividing and gliding and sliding,
And falling and brawling and sprawling,
And driving and riving and striving,
And sprinkling and twinkling and wrinkling,
And sounding and bounding and rounding,
And bubbling and troubling and doubling,
And grumbling and rumbling and tumbling,
And clattering and battering and shattering;

Retreating and beating and meeting and sheeting,
Delaying and straying and playing and spraying,
Advancing and prancing and glancing and dancing,
Recoiling, turmoiling and toiling and boiling,
And gleaming and streaming and steaming and beaming,
And rushing and flushing and brushing and gushing,
And flapping and rapping and clapping and slapping,
And curling and whirling and purling and twirling,
And thumping and plumping and bumping and jumping,
And dashing and flashing and splashing and clashing;
And so never ending, but always descending,
Sounds and motions for ever and ever are blending,
All at once and all o'er, with a mighty uproar;
And this way the water comes down at Lodore.

18.

Sister Susie's sewing shirts for soldiers,
Such skill at sewing shirts our shy young
Sister Susie shows.
Some soldiers send epistles
Say they'd rather sleep in thistles
Than the saucy, soft, short shirts for soldiers
Sister Susie sews.

CHAPTER III

WORDS AND SENTENCES

Vocabularies. The collection of words a person can command either in use or understanding is a vocabulary. Every person has three distinct ones: his reading vocabulary, his writing vocabulary, his speaking vocabulary. Of these, the reading vocabulary is the largest. There are thousands of words he recognizes in reading and although he might not be able to construct a dictionary definition for every one, he has a sufficiently clear idea to grasp the meaning. In this rude approximation to sense he is aided by the context, but for all practical purposes he understands the word. If he were writing, carefully taking time to note exactly what he was expressing, he might recall that word and so consciously put it into a sentence. He might use it in exactly the same sense in which he had seen it in print. But never in the rush of ideas and words in spoken discourse would he risk using a word he knew so slightly. If nothing more, he would beware of mispronunciation.

Thus a person could easily deduce from his reading that a *hangar* is a building to house airplanes. He might—to avoid repeating the word *shed* too frequently—use it in writing. But until he was absolutely certain of its significance and its sound he would hardly venture to say it to other men.

Spoken discourse is so alive, it moves so rapidly, that it is never so precise, so varied in its choice of words, as written material. The phraseology of written discourse sounds slightly or markedly stilted, bookish, if repeated by the tongue. This difference—though it may appear almost trifling—is apparent to everyone. Its recognition can be partly illustrated by the fact that after President Lowell and Senator Lodge had debated on the topic, the League of Nations, in Boston and were shown the reports of their speeches, each made changes in certain expressions. The version for print and reading is a little more formal than the delivered sentences. The Senator said, "I want" but preferred to write "I wish"; then he changed "has got to be" into "must," and "nothing to see" into "nothing visible."

One might say that all three vocabularies should correspond, but there is no real need of this. So long as people read they will meet thousands of words for which they have no need in speaking. Everybody must be able to understand the masterpieces of the past with their archaic (old-fashioned) words like *eftsoons* or *halidom*, but no one need use such expressions now. So there is no discredit in the fact that one's speaking vocabulary is more restricted than his reading vocabulary.

New Ideas, New Words. It is true, however, that an educated person should never rest content with the size of his usable speaking vocabulary. The addition of every new word is likely to indicate the grasp of a new idea. Likewise, every new idea is almost certain to require its individual terms for expression. An enlarging vocabulary is the outward and visible sign of an inward and intellectual growth. No man's vocabulary can equal the size of a dictionary, the latest of which in English is estimated to contain some 450,000 words. Life may be maintained upon a surprisingly meager group of words, as travelers in foreign lands can testify. Shakespeare's vocabulary is said to have included as many as 15,000 words. Figures for that of the average person vary considerably.

Increasing the Vocabulary. The method of increasing a vocabulary is a quite simple process. Its procedure is a fascinating exercise. It covers four steps. When a new word is encountered it should be noticed with keen attention. If heard, its pronunciation will be fixed upon the ear. If seen, its spelling should be mastered at once. The next step is to consult a dictionary for either spelling or pronunciation. Then all its meanings should be examined. Still the word is not yours until you have used it exactly. This you should do at the first opportunity. If the opportunity seems long in coming make it for yourself by discussing with some one the topic with which it was used or frankly discuss the word itself. How many unfamiliar words have you heard or seen recently? How many do you easily use now in your own remarks? You might find it a good plan to take a linguistic inventory every night. A little practice in this will produce amazingly interesting and profitable results in both use and understanding. A keenness for words will be rapidly developed. Word-lists of all kinds will take on entirely new meanings. A spontaneous receptivity will develop into permanent retention of words and phrases.

EXERCISES

1. Tell of some new word you have added to your vocabulary recently. Explain when you met it, how it happened to impress you, what you learned of it.

2. In studying a foreign language how did you fix in your mind the words which permanently stuck there?

3. Look over a page in a dictionary. Report to the class on some interesting material you find.

4. Make a list of ten slang or technical expressions. Explain them in exact, clear language.

5. Find and bring to class a short printed passage, which because of the words, you cannot understand. Unusual books, women's fashion magazines, technical journals, books of rules for games, financial reports, contain good examples.

6. How much do you know about any of the following words?

chassis	fuselage	orthodox	sable
comptometer	germicide	plebescite	self-determination
covenant	layman	purloin	soviet
ethiopian	morale	querulous	vers libre
farce	nectar	renegade	zoom

7. Comment on the words in the following extracts:

"Of enchanting crimson brocade is the slipover blouse which follows the lines of the French cuirasse. Charmingly simple, this blouse, quite devoid of trimming, achieves smartness by concealing the waistline with five graceful folds."

"The shift bid consists in bidding a suit, of which you have little or nothing, with the ultimate object of transferring later to another declaration, which is perfectly sound. The idea is to keep your adversaries from leading this suit up to your hand, which they will likely avoid doing, thinking that you are strong in it."

"While sentiment is radically bearish on corn there is so little pressure on the market other than from shorts that a majority of traders are inclined to go slow in pressing the selling side on breaks until the situation becomes more clearly defined. The weekly forecast for cool weather is regarded as favorable for husking and shelling, and while there was evening up on the part of the pit operators for the double holiday, some of the larger local professionals went home short expecting a lower opening Tuesday."

8. Make a list of ten new words you have learned recently.

Suffixes and Prefixes. Definite steps for continuous additions can be mapped out and covered. Careful attention to prefixes and suffixes will enlarge the vocabulary.

PREFIXES

1. **a** = on, in, at, to; *abed, aboard, afield, afire*

2. **ab (a, abs)** = from, away; *absent, abstract, abdicate*

3. **ad, etc.** = to, in addition to; *adapt, admit, adduce*

4. **ante** = before, *anteroom, antebellum*

5. **anti** = against, opposite; *anticlimax, antipodes, antipathy*

6. **bi**= two; *bicycle, biennial, biped, biplane*

7. **circum** = around, about; *circumnavigate, circumscribe, circumvent*

8. **con (col, com, co, cor, etc.)** = with, together; *consent, collect, coördinate, composite, conspiracy*

9. **contra (counter)** = against; *contradict, counteract, countermand*

10. **de** = down, from, away; *depose, desist, decapitate, denatured*

11. **demi, hemi, semi** = half; *demi-tasse, hemisphere, semiannual, semitransparent*

12. **di** (**dis**) = twice, double; *dissyllable*

13. **dis** (**di**, **dif**) = apart, away, not; *distract, diverge, diversion, disparage*

14. **en** (**em**) = in, on, into; *engrave, embody, embrace*

15. **extra** = beyond; *extraordinary, extravagant*

16. **hyper** = above; *hypercritical*

17. **in** (**il**, **im**, **ir**) = in, into, not; *inclose, illustrate, irrigate, inform, illiterate, impious, irregular*

18. **ex** (**e**, **ec**, **ef**) = out of, from, beyond, thoroughly, formerly but not now; *exclude, excel, ex-senator.*

19. **inter** = between, among; *intercede, interchange, interfere, interurban, interlude*

20. **mis** = wrongly, badly; *miscalculate, misspell, misadventure*

21. **mono** = one; *monoplane*

22. **per** = through, thoroughly, by; *perchance, perfect, per-adventure*

23. **poly** = many; *polygon, polytheism*

24. **post** = behind, after; *postgraduate, post-mortem, postlude, postscript, post-meridian* (P.M.)

25. **pre** = before (in time, place, or order); *preëminent, predict, prefer, prefix, prejudge, prejudice*

26. **preter** = beyond; *preternatural*

27. **pro** = before, forth, forward; *proceed, prosecute*

28. **pro** = siding with; *pro-ally*

29. **re** = back, again; *recover, renew, recall*

30. **sub**, etc. = under; *submerge, subscribe, subterranean, subterfuge*

31. **super** (**sur**) = over, above; *superintend, supercargo*

32. **trans** (**tra**) = across; *translate, transmit, transfer*

33. **vice** (**vis**) = instead of; *vice-president, vice-admiral*

SUFFIXES

1. **ee**, **er** = one who; *absentee, profiteer, mower*

2. **ard**, **art**= term of disparagement; *drunkard, braggart*

3. **esque** = like; *statuesque*

4. **ism** = state of being; *barbarism, atheism*

5. **et**, **let** = little; *brooklet, bracelet, eaglet*

6. **ling** = little, young; *duckling, gosling*

7. **kin** = little; *lambkin, Peterkin*

8. **stead** = a place; *bedstead, homestead, instead*

9. **wright** = a workman; *wheelwright*

Thesaurus. Besides frequently consulting a good modern dictionary a student speaker should familiarize himself with a *Thesaurus* of words and phrases. This is a peculiarly useful compilation of expressions according to their meaning relations. A dictionary lists words, then gives their meanings. A Thesaurus arranges meanings, then gives the words that express those ideas. The value of such a book can be best illustrated by explaining its use.

Suppose a speaker is going to attack some principle, some act, some party. He knows that his main theme will be denunciation of something. In the index of a Thesaurus he looks under *denunciation*, finding two numbers of paragraphs. Turning to the first he has under his eye a group of words all expressing shades of this idea. There are further references to other related terms. Let us look at the first group, taken from Roget's *Thesaurus*.

> MALEDICTON, curse, imprecation, denunciation, execration, anathema, ban, proscription, excommunication, commination, fulmination.

Cursing, scolding, railing, Billingsgate language.

V. To curse, accurse, imprecate, scold, rail, execrate.

To denounce, proscribe, excommunicate, fulminate.

Adj. Cursing, &c., cursed, &c.

THREAT, menace, defiance, abuse, commination, intimidation.

V. To threaten, menace, defy, fulminate; to intimidate.

Adj. Threatening, menacing, minatory, abusive.

The second reference leads us farther. It presents the expressions dealing with the methods and results of *denunciation*, providing hundreds of words and phrases to use in various ways. It does even more, for in a parallel column it gives a list of opposites for the words indicating *condemnation*. This more than doubles its value. Finally having reached the word *punishment* it lists its cognates until the idea *penalty* is reached, where it balances that idea with *reward* and its synonyms. A portion of this section follows.

LAWSUIT, suit, action, cause, trial, litigation.

Denunciation, citation, arraignment, persecution, indictment, impeachment, apprehension, arrest, committal, imprisonment.

Pleadings, writ, summons, plea, bill, affidavit, &c.

Verdict, sentence, judgment, finding, decree, arbitrament, adjudication, award.

V. To go to law; to take the law of; to appeal to the law; to join issue; file a bill, file a claim.

To denounce, cite, apprehend, arraign, sue, prosecute, bring to trial, indict, attach, distrain, to commit, give in charge or custody; throw into prison.

To try, hear a cause, sit in judgment.

To pronounce, find, judge, sentence, give judgment; bring in a verdict; doom, to arbitrate, adjudicate, award, report.

ACQUITTAL, absolution, *see* Pardon, 918, clearance, discharge, release, reprieve, respite.

Exemption from punishment; impunity.

V. To acquit, absolve, clear, discharge, release, reprieve, respite.

Adj. Acquitted, &c.

Uncondemned, unpunished, unchastised.

CONDEMNATION, conviction, proscription; death warrant.

Attainder, attainment.

V. To condemn, convict, cast, find guilty, proscribe.

Adj. Condemnatory, &c.

PUNISHMENT, chastisement, castigation, correction, chastening, discipline, infliction, etc.

An observer will see at once just how far these lists go and what must supplement them. They do not define, they do not discriminate, they do not restrict. They are miscellaneous collections. A person must consult the dictionary or refer to some other authority to prevent error or embarrassment in use. For instance, under the entry *newspaper* occurs the attractive word *ephemeris*. But one should be careful of how and where he uses that word.

Another exercise which will aid in fixing both words and meanings in the mind and also help in the power of recalling them for instant use is to make some kind of word-list according to some principle or scheme. One plan might be to collect all the words dealing with the idea of *book*. Another might be to take some obvious word root and then follow it and other roots added to it through all its forms, meanings, and uses. One might choose *tel* (distant) and *graph* (record) and start with *telegraph*. *Telephone* will introduce *phone, phonograph*; they will lead on to *dictaphone, dictagraph*;

the first half links with *dictation*; that may lead as far away as *dictatorial*. In fact there is no limit to the extent, the interest, and the value of these various exercises. The single aim of all of them should be, of course, the enlargement of the speaking vocabulary. Mere curiosities, current slang, far-fetched metaphors, passing foreign phrases, archaisms, obsolete and obsolescent terms, too new coinages, atrocities, should be avoided as a plague.

Consistent, persistent, insistent word-study is of inestimable value to a speaker. And since all people speak, it follows that it would benefit everybody.

EXERCISES

1. Explain what is meant by each entry in the foregoing list.

2. List some verbal curiosities you have met recently. Examples: "Mr. Have-it-your-own-way is the best husband." "He shows a great deal of stick-to-it-iveness."

3. What should be the only condition for using foreign expressions? Can you show how foreign words become naturalized? Cite some foreign words used in speech.

4. Are archaic (old-fashioned), obsolete (discarded), and obsolescent (rapidly disappearing) terms more common in speech or books? Explain and illustrate.

Synonyms. As has already been suggested, a copious vocabulary must not be idle in a person's equipment. He must be able to use it. He must be able to discriminate as to meaning. This power of choosing the exact word results from a study of synonyms. It is a fact that no two words mean *exactly* the same thing. No matter how nearly alike the two meanings may appear to be, closer consideration will unfailingly show at least a slight difference of dignity, if nothing more—as *red* and *crimson*, *pure* and *unspotted*. Synonyms, then, are groups of words whose meanings are almost the same. These are the words which give so much trouble to learners of our language. A foreigner is told that *stupid* means *dull*, yet he is corrected if he says *a stupid knife*. Many who learn English as a native tongue fail to comprehend the many delicate shades of differences among synonyms.

In this matter, also, a dictionary goes so far as to list synonyms, and in some cases, actually adds a discussion to define the various limits. For fuller, more careful discrimination a good book of synonyms should be consulted. Except for some general consideration of words which everyone is certain to use or misuse, it is better to consult a treatise on synonyms when need arises than to study it consecutively. In consultation the material will be fixed by instant use. In study it may fade before being employed; it may never be required.

The subjoined paragraphs show entries in two different volumes upon synonyms:

> Adjacent, adjoining, contiguous. Adjacent, in Latin, *adjiciens*, participle of *adjicio*, is compounded of *ad* and *jacio*, to lie near. *Adjoining*, as the word implies, signifies being joined together. Contiguous, in French *contigu*, Latin *contiguus*, comes from *contingo*, or *con* and *tango*, signifying to touch close.
>
> What is *adjacent* may be separated altogether by the intervention of some third object; what is *adjoining* must touch in some part; and what is *contiguous* must be fitted to touch entirely on one side. Lands are *adjacent* to a house or town; fields are *adjoining* to each other; and houses *contiguous* to each other.
>
> CRABBE: *English Synonyms*
>
> Victory: Synonyms: achievement, advantage, conquest, mastery, success, supremacy, triumph. *Victory* is the state resulting from the overcoming of an opponent or opponents in any contest, or from the overcoming of difficulties, obstacles, evils, etc., considered as opponents or enemies. In the latter sense any hard-won *achievement*, *advantage*, or *success* may be termed a victory. In *conquest* and *mastery* there is implied a permanence of state that is not implied in *victory*. *Triumph*, originally denoting the public rejoicing in honor of a *victory*, has come to

signify also a peculiarly exultant, complete, and glorious *victory*. Compare *conquer*. Antonyms: defeat, destruction, disappointment, disaster, failure, frustration, miscarriage, overthrow, retreat, rout.

FERNALD: English Synonyms, Antonyms and Prepositions

Antonyms. Notice that this second paragraph adds a new word-list—*antonyms*. To reinforce the understanding of what a thing is, it is desirable to know what it is not, or what its opposite is. This kind of explanation or description is especially valuable to a speaker. He can frequently impress an audience more definitely by explaining the opposite of what he wants them to apprehend. At times the term is not the extreme opposite; it is merely the negative of the other. Logically the other side of *white* is *not white*, while the antonym is the extreme *black*. Trained speakers use with great effect the principle underlying such groups of words. When Burke argued before the House of Commons for a plan to secure harmony with the American colonies he described the scheme he considered necessary by showing what it should not be. "No partial, narrow, contracted, pinched, occasional system will be at all suitable to such an object." Describing the peace he hoped would be secured he used this principle of opposites. "Not peace through the medium of war; not peace to be hunted through the labyrinth of intricate and endless negotiations, not peace to arise out of universal discord, fomented from principle in all parts of the empire; not peace to depend on the juridical determination of perplexing questions, or the precise marking the shadowy boundaries of a complex government."

We are told by an investigator that one of the reasons for a Frenchman's keen insight into the capabilities of his language is the early training received in schools covering differences among words. This continual weighing of the meaning or the suitability of an expression is bound to result in a delicate appreciation of its value as a means of effective communication. In all mental action the sense of contrast is an especially lively one. In a later chapter this principle, as applied to explanation and argument, will be discussed. Just here, the point is that the constant study of contrasts will sharpen the language sense and rapidly enlarge the vocabulary.

EXERCISES

1. Put down a group of five words having similar meanings. Explain the differences among them.

2. Choose any word. Give its exact opposite.

3. From any short paragraph copy all the nouns. In a parallel column put opposites or contrasts.

4. Do the same for the adjectives, verbs, and adverbs.

5. Write down all the common nouns which correspond to *a man, a girl, a leader, a house, a costume, a crime.*

Composition of the English Language. Turning now from the means of improving the speaker's language equipment let us pass to some remarks upon his use of words. The English language is the largest, the most varied in the universe. Almost entirely free from difficulties of inflection and conjugation, with a simplified grammar, and a great freedom of construction, it suffers from only two signal drawbacks—its spelling and its pronunciation. While it has preserved to a great degree its original Anglo-Saxon grammar, it has enriched its vocabulary by borrowings from everywhere. Its words have no distinctive forms, so every foreign word can usually be naturalized by a mere change of sound. No matter what their origin, all belong to one family now; *gnu* is as much English as *knew, japan* as *pogrom, fête* as *papoose, batik* as *radii, ohm* as *marconigram, macadamized* as *zoomed*. Most of the modern borrowings—as just illustrated—were to serve for new things or ideas. But there was one time when a great reduplication of the vocabulary occurred. After the French conquered England in 1066, English and Norman-French were spoken side by side. The resultant tongue, composed of both, offered many doubles for the same idea. In some instances the fashionable and aristocratic French word marked a difference of meaning as is clearly indicated by such pairs as *beef* and *ox, veal* and *calf, mutton* and *sheep, pork* and *pig*. In many other cases words of French and English origin are separated by differences less distinct. Such are *love* and *affection, worship* and *adoration*. A speaker must take thought of such groups, and consciously endeavor to use the more appropriate for his purpose.

Anglo-Saxon and Romance. It may help him to remember that the Anglo-Saxon words are the more homely, the closer to our everyday feelings and experiences, the expression of our deepest ideas and sentiments, the natural outspoken response to keen emotion. On the other hand, the Romance words—as they are called, whether from the French or directly from the Latin—are likely to be longer; they belong generally to the more complicated relationships of society and government; they are more intellectual in the sense that they represent the operations of the brain rather than the impulses of the heart. They deal with more highly trained wills, with more abstruse problems; they reason, they argue, they consider; they are philosophical, scientific, legal, historical. Listen to a soldier relate his war experiences. What will his vocabulary be? Listen to a diplomat explaining the League of Nations. What will his vocabulary be? Have you ever heard a speaker who gave you the impression that all his words ended in *tion*? This was because his vocabulary was largely Romance.

The inferences from the foregoing are perfectly plain. Subject and audience will determine to a large extent what kinds of words a speaker will choose. The well-equipped speaker will be master of both kinds; he will draw from either as occasion offers. He will not insult one audience by talking below their intelligence, nor will he bore another by speaking over their heads.

General and Specific Terms. Effective speaking depends to a large extent upon the inclusion of specific terms as contrasted with general terms. "Glittering generalities" never make people listen. They mean nothing because they say too much. Study the following selections to see how the concrete phraseology used makes the material more telling, how it enforces the meaning. Pick out the best expressions and explain why they are better than more general terms. In the first, note how the last sentence drives home the meaning of the first two. Listeners may understand the first two, they remember the last.

> Civil and religious liberty in this country can be preserved only through the agency of our political institutions. But those institutions alone will not suffice. It is not the ship so much as the skilful sailing that assures the prosperous voyage.

GEORGE WILLIAM CURTIS: *The Public Duty of Educated Men,*
1877

Describe the significance of the best expressions in the following speech made in Parliament by Thomas Babington Macaulay.

> All those fierce spirits whom you hallooed on to harass us now turn round and begin to worry you. The Orangeman raises his war-whoop; Exeter Hall sets up its bray; Mr. Macneill shudders to see more costly cheer than ever provided for the Priest of Baal at the table of the Queen; and the Protestant operatives of Dublin call for impeachments in exceedingly bad English. But what did you expect? Did you think when, to serve your turn, you called the devil up that it was as easy to lay him as to raise him? Did you think when you went on, session after session, thwarting and reviling those whom you knew to be in the right, and flattering all the worst passions of those whom you knew to be in the wrong, that the day of reckoning would never come? It has come. There you sit, doing penance for the disingenuousness of years.

Why was the style of the extract below especially good for the evident purpose and audience? Why did the author use names for the candidates?

> When an American citizen is content with voting merely, he consents to accept what is often a doubtful alternative. His first duty is to help shape the alternative. This, which was formerly less necessary, is now indispensable. In a rural community such as this country was a hundred years-ago, whoever was nominated for office was known to his neighbors, and the consciousness of that knowledge was a conservative influence in determining nominations. But in the local elections of the great cities of today, elections that control taxation and expenditure, the mass of the voters vote in absolute ignorance of the candidates. The citizen who supposes that he does all his duty when he votes, places a premium upon political knavery. Thieves welcome him to the polls and offer him a choice, which he has done nothing to prevent, between Jeremy Diddler and

Dick Turpin. The party cries for which he is responsible are: "Turpin and Honesty," "Diddler and Reform." And within a few years, as a result of this indifference to the details of public duty, the most powerful politicians in the Empire State of the Union was Jonathan Wild, the Great, the captain of a band of plunderers.

GEORGE WILLIAM CURTIS: *The Public Duty of Educated Men*,
1877

Appropriate Diction. The final test of any diction is its appropriateness. The man who talks of dignified things as he would of a baseball game— unless he is doing it deliberately for humor, caricature, or burlesque—is ruining his own cause. The man who discusses trifles in the style of philosophy makes himself an egregious bore. As Shakespeare said, "Suit the action to the word, the word to the action; with this special observance, that you o'erstep not the modesty of nature."

Beware of the flowery expression; avoid metaphorical speech; flee from the lure of the overwrought style. In the first place it is so old-fashioned that audiences suspect it at once. It fails to move them. It may plunge its user into ridiculous failure. In the excitement of spontaneous composition a man sometimes takes risks. He may—as Pitt is reported to have said he did— throw himself into a sentence and trust to God Almighty to get him out. But a beginner had better walk before he tries to soar. If he speaks surely rather than amazingly his results will be better. The temptation to leave the ground is ever present in speaking.

A Parliamentary debater describing the Church of England wound up in a flowery conclusion thus: "I see the Church of England rising in the land, with one foot firmly planted in the soil, the other stretched toward Heaven!"

An American orator discussing the character of Washington discharged the following.

The higher we rise in the scale of being—material, intellectual, and moral—the more certainly we quit the region of the brilliant eccentricities and dazzling contrasts which belong to a vulgar greatness. Order and proportion characterize the primordial constitution of the terrestrial system; ineffable harmony rules the heavens. All the great eternal forces act in solemn silence. The brawling torrent that dries up in summer deafens you with its roaring whirlpools in March; while the vast earth on which we dwell, with all its oceans and all its continents and its thousand millions of inhabitants, revolves unheard upon its soft axle at the rate of a thousand miles an hour, and rushes noiselessly on its orbit a million and a half miles a day. Two storm-clouds encamped upon opposite hills on a sultry summer's evening, at the expense of no more electricity, according to Mr. Faraday, than is evolved in the decomposition of a single drop of water, will shake the surrounding atmosphere with their thunders, which, loudly as they rattle on the spot, will yet not be heard at the distance of twenty miles; while those tremendous and unutterable forces which ever issue from the throne of God, and drag the chariot wheels of Uranus and Neptune along the uttermost path-ways of the solar system, pervade the illimitable universe in silence.

Of course, today, nobody talks like that. At least no one should.

Trite Expressions. Less easily guarded against is the delivery of trite expressions. These are phrases and clauses which at first were so eloquent that once heard they stuck in people's minds, who then in an endeavor themselves to be emphatic inserted continually into their speeches these overworked, done-to-death expressions, which now having been used too frequently have no real meaning. One of the most frequently abused is "of the people, by the people, for the people." Others are words and phrases made popular by the war. Many are no more than jargon—meaningless counterfeits instead of the legal tender of real speech. It is amazing to notice how persistently some of them recur in the remarks of apparently well-trained men who should know better than to insert them. The following were used by a prominent United States political leader in a single speech.

He could; easily have replaced them by living material or dispensed with them entirely.

> Jot or tittle; the plain unvarnished truth; God forbid; the jackal press; that memorable occasion; tooth and nail; the God of our fathers; the awful horrors of Valley Forge; the blood-stained heights of Yorktown; tell it not in Gath; proclaim it not in the streets of Askalon; peace with honor; the Arabian Nights; Munchausen; the fathers; our globe-encircling domain; I am a Democrat; the pirates of the Barbary Coast; Democratic gospel pure and undefiled; Janus-faced double; Good Lord, good devil; all things to all men; God-fearing patriots; come what may; all things are fair in love or war; the silken bowstring; the unwary voter; bait to catch gudgeons; to live by or to die by; these obsequious courtiers; Guttenburg; rubber stamp; at all hazards; the most unkindest cut of all.

With the artificiality, the stiltedness of the foregoing contrast the simplicity, the sincerity of these two extracts from Abraham Lincoln.

> And now, if they would listen—as I suppose they will not—I would address a few words to the Southern people.

> I would say to them: You consider yourselves a reasonable and a just people; and I consider that in the general qualities of reason and justice you are not inferior to any other people. Still, when you speak of us Republicans, you do so only to denounce us as reptiles, or, at the best, as no better than outlaws. You will grant a hearing to pirates or murderers, but nothing like it to "Black Republicans." In all your contentions with one another, each of you deems an unconditional condemnation of "Black Republicanism" as the first thing to be attended to. Indeed, such condemnation of us seems to be an indispensable prerequisite— license, so to speak—among you to be admitted or permitted to speak at all. Now can you or not be prevailed upon to pause and to consider whether this is quite just to us, or even to yourselves? Bring forward your charges and specifications, and then be patient long enough to hear us deny or justify.

My Friends: No one, not in my situation, can appreciate my feeling of sadness at this parting. To this place, and the kindness of these people, I owe everything. Here I have lived a quarter of a century, and have passed from a young to an old man. Here my children have been born, and one is buried. I now leave, not knowing when or whether ever I may return, with a task before me greater than that which rested upon Washington. Without the assistance of that Divine Being who ever attended him, I cannot succeed. With that assistance I cannot fail. Trusting in Him who can go with me, and remain with you, and be everywhere for good, let us confidently hope that all will yet be well. To His care commending you, as I hope in your prayers you will commend me, I bid you an affectionate farewell.

Farewell Address at Springfield, 1861

Kinds of Sentences. What kinds of sentences shall a speaker construct as he speaks? That there is a difference between those a person composes when he writes and those the same person is likely to evolve when he speaks is realized by everyone. We hear that a speaker is "booky," or conversational, that he is stilted or lively, that he is too formal, that his discourse is dull and flat. To a great degree these criticisms are based upon the sentence structure.

The Simple Sentence. The simple sentence contains only one subject and one predicate. The complex sentence contains one independent clause and at least one subordinate clause. The compound sentence contains two or more independent clauses. It would be good advice to urge the employment of the simple sentence were it not for the fact that a long succession of sentences constructed exactly alike, making the same impression of form and sound and length, is likely to produce a deadly monotony of emphasis and pause, an impression of immaturity on the part of the speaker and of lack of skill in molding his phrases. Yet, in the main, the simple sentence is a valuable kind to know how to deliver. Containing but a single thought it is likely to make a definite impression upon a listener. It offers him not too much to grasp. It leads him a single step along the way. It speaks clearly, concisely. Its advantages follow from its qualities. At the beginning of addresses it is especially efficient in leading the audience at the same rate—slowly, it should be—as the speaker. In intricate explanation, in close reasoning, in matters of paramount importance, it should be employed.

Management of the short, simple sentence in written prose is difficult. In spoken discourse, as well, it is so easy to fall into the First Primer style that while the advantages of the use of the simple sentence are great, the ability to produce good sentences in succession must be developed.

The Complex Sentence. The complex sentence offers a good form for introducing pertinent, minor details, which are necessary, yet which do not merit inclusion in the general level of the speech. Aided by proper pitch and inflection of the voice, they can be skilfully subordinated to main ideas, yet introduced so adroitly that they at times relieve attention, at others briefly explain, at others keep adding up in a series the effect of which is a large total. Frequently such sentences indicate clearly the progress of the discussion. A topic introduced in a subordinate clause may later be raised to more importance without abruptness, for hearers are already familiar with it. A topic already treated may be recalled by citation in a later clause. So various parts of a speech may be closely knit together to present a coherent, progressive, unified whole.

In easily grasped general, descriptive, narrative, explanatory material, complex sentences will allow the covering of a wide field, or a long time, in short order by condensing facts into the few words of subordinate clauses.

The Compound Sentence. Somewhat like the use of complex sentences for general material is the use of compound ones for informal topics, familiar discourse, easy address, lighter material. Valuable, too, is this form for the speaker who knows accurately the meaning of conjunctions, who can avoid the stringing together of what should be simple sentences by a dozen senseless *ands.* A good rule for the beginner is to allow no *ands* in his speeches except those so imbedded in phrases—husband and wife, now and then, principal and interest—that he cannot avoid them. Let him never speak such sentences as, "I came to this meeting and discovered only when I got here that I was scheduled to speak." Let him be careful of beginning sentence's with *and* after he has made a pause.

The Exclamatory Sentence. Many speakers yield to the temptation to strive for effect by delivering exclamatory sentences—sometimes only clauses and phrases so enunciated. The disposition to do this is born of the desire to be emphatic. Strong feeling makes one burst out in ejaculation. Used sparingly this form may be extremely effective. Used too frequently it reduces a speech to a mere series of ejaculations of little more value than a succession of grunts, groans, and sobs. Exclamatory sentences seldom convey much meaning. They indicate emotion. But a speech, to be worth listening to, must convey ideas.

The Interrogative Sentence. A second sentence which may be classed with the preceding is the interrogative. There is a disposition on the part of speakers to ask direct questions of the audience. Frequently the rhetorical question—which is one asked because the answer is the quite apparent fact the speaker wants to impress upon his hearers—is an effective method of making a seemingly personal appeal to sluggish intellects or lazy wills. The interrogative form has the same disadvantage as the exclamatory. Except when its answer is perfectly plain it transfers no meaning. It would be easily possible for a speaker with no ideas at all, no knowledge of a topic, to engage time and attention by merely constructing a series of questions. At the conclusion the audience would wonder why in the world he spoke, for he had so little to say.

Long and Short Sentences. So far as long and short sentences are concerned some general rules have already been hinted at in dealing with other kinds. The advantages of the short sentence are mainly those of clearness, directness, emphasis. Its dangers are monotony, bareness, over-compactness. The advantages of the long—that is, quite long—sentence, are rather difficult to comprehend. A wordy sentence is likely to defeat its own purpose. Instead of guiding it will lose its hearer. Somewhat long sentences—as already said—will serve in general discussions, in rapidly moving descriptive and narrative passages, in rather simple explanation and argument. No one can state at just what number of words a short sentence becomes medium, and when the division of medium becomes long. Yet there must be some limits. A sentence in *Les Misérables* includes nearly one thousand words in both French original and English translation. John Milton produced some extraordinarily long sentences. But these are in written discourse. Some modern speakers have come dangerously near the limit. In one printed speech one sentence has four hundred ten words in it; a later one goes to five hundred forty. This second would fill about half a column of the usual newspaper. Surely these are much too long. A speaker can frequently make a long sentence acceptable by breaking it up into shorter elements by sensible pauses. Yet the general direction must surely be: avoid sentences which are too long.

Variety. The paramount rule of sentence structure in speech-making is certainly: secure variety. Long, medium, short; declarative, exclamatory, interrogative; simple, loose, periodic; use them all as material permits and economy of time and attention prescribes. With the marvelous variety possible in English sentence structure, no person with ideas and language at command need be a monotonous speaker.

EXERCISES

1. Criticize this selection for its diction and sentence structure. What excellences has it? What can you find fault with? Does its date explain it?

> "The books in the library, the portraits, the table at which he wrote, the scientific culture of the land, the course of agricultural occupation, the coming-in of harvests, fruit of the seed his own hand had scattered, the animals and implements of husbandry, the trees planted by him in lines, in copses, in orchards by thousands, the seat under the noble elm on which he used to sit to feel the southwest wind at evening, or hear the breathings of the sea, or the not less audible music of the starry heavens, all seemed at first unchanged. The sun of a bright day from which, however, something of the fervors of midsummer were wanting, fell temperately on them all, filled the air on all sides with the utterances of life, and gleamed on the long line of ocean. Some of those whom on earth he loved best, still were there. The great mind still seemed to preside; the great presence to be with you; you might expect to hear again the rich and playful tones of the voice of the old hospitality. Yet a moment more, and all the scene took on the aspect of one great monument, inscribed with his name, and sacred to his memory. And such it shall be in all the future of America! The sensation

of desolateness, and loneliness, and darkness, with which you see it now, will pass away; the sharp grief of love and friendship will become soothed; men will repair thither as they are wont to commemorate the great days of history; the same glance shall take in, and same emotions shall greet and bless, the Harbor of the Pilgrims and the Tomb of Webster."

Rufus Choate: *A Discourse Commemorative of Daniel Webster,* 1853

2. What is the effect of the questions in the following? Are the sentences varied? If the occasion was momentous, what is the style?

"And judging by the past, I wish to know what there has been in the conduct of the British ministry for the last ten years, to justify those hopes with which gentlemen have been pleased to solace themselves and the house? Is it that insidious smile with which our petition has been lately received? Trust it not, Sir; it will prove a snare to your feet. Suffer not yourselves to be betrayed with a kiss. Ask yourselves how this gracious reception of our petition comports with those warlike preparations which cover our water and darken our land. Are fleets and armies necessary to a work of love and reconciliation? Have we shown ourselves so unwilling to be reconciled that force must be called in to win back our love?"

Patrick Henry: *Speech in the Virginia Convention,* 1775

3. List the concrete details given below. What effect have they? What elements give the idea of the extent of the Colonies' fisheries? Are the sentences long or short? Does their success justify them?

"Look at the manner in which the people of New England have of late carried on the whale fishery. Whilst we follow them among the tumbling mountains of ice, and behold them penetrating into the deepest frozen recess of Hudson's Bay and Davis' Straits, whilst we are looking for them beneath the arctic circle, we hear that they have pierced into the opposite region of polar cold, that they are at the antipodes, and engaged under the frozen Serpent of the South. Falkland Islands, which seemed too remote and romantic an object for the grasp of national ambition, is but a stage and resting-place in the progress of their victorious industry. Nor is the equinoctial heat more discouraging to them than the accumulated winter of both the poles. We know that whilst some of them draw the line and strike the harpoon on the coast of Africa, others run the longitude and pursue their gigantic game along the coast of Brazil. No sea but what is vexed by their fisheries; no climate that is not witness to their toil. Neither the perseverance of Holland, nor the activity of France, nor the dexterous and firm sagacity of English enterprise ever carried this most perilous mode of hardy industry to the extent to which it has been pushed by, this recent people; a people who are still, as it were, but in the gristle, and not yet hardened into the bone of manhood."

EDMUND BURKE: Conciliation with America, 1775

4. Is the following clear? What kind of sentence is it? What minor phrase? Is this phrase important? Why? Why did Lincoln repeat this sentence, practically with no change, twelve times in a single speech?

"The sum of the whole is that of our thirty-nine fathers who framed the original Constitution, twenty-one—a clear majority of the whole—certainly understood that no proper division of local from Federal authority, nor any part of the Constitution, forbade the Federal Government to control slavery in the Federal Territories."

ABRAHAM LINCOLN: Cooper Union Speech, 1860

5. Is the following well phrased? What makes it so? Is any expression too strong? Do you object to any? How many of the words would you be likely not to use?

"It is but too true that there are many whose whole scheme of freedom is made up of pride, perverseness, and insolence. They feel themselves in a state of thraldom; they imagine that their souls are cooped and cabined in, unless they have some man, or some body of men, dependent on their mercy. The desire of having some one below them descends to those who are the very lowest of all; and a Protestant cobbler, debased by his poverty, but exalted by his share of the ruling church, feels a pride in knowing it is by his generosity alone that the peer, whose footman's instep he measures, is able to keep his chaplain from a gaol. This disposition is the true source of the passion which many men, in very humble life, have taken to the American war. Our subjects in America; our colonies; our dependents. This lust of party power is the liberty they hunger and thirst for; and this Siren song of ambition has charmed ears that we would have thought were never organized to that sort of music."

EDMUND BURKE: *Speech at Bristol*, 1780

6. Describe the effects of the questions in the next. How is sentence variety secured? What effects have the simple, declarative sentences?

"And from what have these consequences sprung? We have been involved in no war. We have been at peace with all the world. We have been visited with no national calamity. Our people have been advancing in general intelligence, and, I will add, as great and alarming as has been the advance of political corruption among the mercenary corps who look to government for support, the morals and virtue of the community at large have been advancing in improvement. What, I again repeat, is the cause?"

JOHN C. CALHOUN: *Speech on the Force Bill*, 1833

7. What quality predominates in the following? Does it lower the tone of the passage too much? Is the interrogative form of the last sentence better than the declarative? Why? Has the last observation any close connection with the preceding portion? Can it be justified?

"Modesty is a lovely trait, which sets the last seal to a truly great character, as the blush of innocence adds the last charm to youthful beauty. When, on his return from one of his arduous campaigns in the Seven Years' War, the Speaker of the Virginia

Assembly, by order of the House, addressed Colonel Washington in acknowledgment of his services, the youthful hero rose to reply; but humility checked his utterance, diffidence sealed his lips. 'Sit down, Colonel Washington,' said the Speaker; 'the House sees that your modesty is equal to your merit, and that exceeds my power of language to describe.' But who ever heard of a modest Alexander or a modest Caesar, or a modest hero or statesman of the present day?—much as some of them would be improved by a measure of that quality."

EDWARD EVERETT: Character of Washington, 1858

8. Look up the meaning of every unfamiliar expression in this extract. Is the quotation at the end in good taste? Give reasons for your answer. For what kinds of audiences would this speech be fitting?

"The remedy for the constant excess of party spirit lies, and lies alone, in the courageous independence of the individual citizen. The only way, for instance, to procure the party nomination of good men, is for every self-respecting voter to refuse to vote for bad men. In the medieval theology the devils feared nothing so much as the drop of holy water and the sign of the cross, by which they were exorcised. The evil spirits of party fear nothing so much as bolting and scratching. *In hoc signo vinces*. If a farmer would reap a good crop, he scratches the weeds out of his field. If we would have good men upon the ticket, we must scratch bad men off. If the scratching breaks down the party, let it break: for the success of the party, by such means would break down the country. The evil spirits must be taught by means that they can understand. 'Them fellers,' said the captain of a canal-boat of his men, 'Them fellers never think you mean a thing until you kick 'em. They feel that, and understand.'"

GEORGE WILLIAM CURTIS: The Public Duty of Educated Men,
1877

9. Describe the quality of the next extract. What is its style? Are repetitions allowable? What then of variety? Point out contrasts of words and phrases.

"What, then it is said, would you legislate in haste? Would you legislate in times of great excitement concerning matters of such deep concern? Yes, Sir, I would; and if any bad consequences should follow from the haste and excitement, let those be answerable who, when there was no need to haste, when there existed no excitement, refused to listen to any project of reform; nay, made it an argument against reform that the public mind was not excited.... I allow that hasty legislation is an evil. But reformers are compelled to legislate fast, just because bigots will not legislate early. Reformers are compelled to legislate in times of excitement, because bigots will not legislate in times of tranquillity."

THOMAS BABINGTON MACAULAY: *On the Reform Bill*, 1832

10. Describe the diction of the next extract. Describe the prevailing kind of sentences. Do you approve of these in such an instance? Explain your answer. Does it remind you—in tone—of any other passage already quoted in this book? What is your opinion of the style?

"There has been a change of government. It began two years ago, when the House of Representatives became Democratic by a decisive majority. It has now been completed. The Senate about to assemble will also be Democratic. The offices of President and Vice-President have been put into the hands of Democrats. What does the change mean? That is the question that is uppermost in our minds today. That is the question I am going to try to answer in order, if I may, to interpret the occasion.

"This is not a day of triumph; it is a day of dedication. Here muster, not the forces of party, but the forces of humanity. Men's hearts wait upon us; men's lives hang in the balance; men's hopes call upon us to say what we will do. Who shall live up to the great trust? Who dares fail to try? I summon all honest men, all patriotic, all forward-looking men to my side. God helping me, I will not fail them, if they will but counsel and sustain me."

WOODROW WILSON: *Inaugural*, 1918

11. Consider sentence length in the following: Which words are significant? How is concreteness secured?

"Ours is a government of liberty by, through, and under the law. No man is above it and no man is below it. The crime of cunning, the crime of greed, the crime of violence, are all equally crimes, and against them all alike the law must set its face. This is not and never shall be a government either of plutocracy or of a mob. It is, it has been, and it will be a government of the people; including alike the people of great wealth, of moderate wealth, the people who employ others, the people who are employed, the wage worker, the lawyer, the mechanic, the banker, the farmer; including them all, protecting each and everyone if he acts decently and squarely, and discriminating against any one of them, no matter from what class he comes, if he does not act squarely and fairly, if he does not obey the law. While all people are foolish if they violate or rail against the law, wicked as well as foolish, but all foolish— yet the most foolish man in this Republic is the man of wealth who complains because the law is administered with impartial justice against or for him. His folly is greater than the folly of any other man who so complains; for he lives and moves and has his being because the law does in fact protect him and his property."

THEODORE ROOSEVELT at Spokane, 1903

CHAPTER IV

BEGINNING THE SPEECH

Speech-making a Formal Matter. Every speech is more or less a formal affair. The speaker standing is separated from the other persons present by his prominence. He is removed from them by standing while they sit, by being further away from them than in ordinary conversation. The greater the distance between him and his listeners the more formal the proceeding becomes. When a person speaks "from the floor" as it is called, that is, by simply rising at his seat and speaking, there is a marked difference in the manner of his delivery and also in the effect upon the audience. In many gatherings, speeches and discussions "from the floor" are not allowed at all, in others this practice is the regular method of conducting business. Even in the schoolroom when the student speaks from his place he feels less responsibility than when he stands at the front of the room before his classmates. As all formal exercises have their regular rules of procedure it will be well to list the more usual formulas for beginnings of speeches.

The Salutation. In all cases where speeches are made there is some person who presides. This person may be the Vice-President of the United States presiding over the Senate, the Speaker of the House of Representatives, the Chief Justice of the United States Supreme Court, the president of a city board of aldermen, the judge of a court, the president of a corporation, of a lodge, of a church society, of a club, the pastor of a church, the chancellor or provost or dean of a college, the principal of a school, the chairman of a committee, the toastmaster of a banquet, the teacher of a class. The first remark of a speaker must always be the recognition of this presiding officer.

Then there are frequently present other persons who are distinct from the ordinary members of the audience, to whom some courtesy should be shown in this salutation. Their right to recognition depends upon their rank, their importance at the time, some special peculiar reason for separating them from the rest of the audience. The speaker will have to decide for himself in most cases as to how far he will classify his hearers. In some instances there is no difficulty. Debaters must recognize the presiding officer, the judges if they be distinct from the regular audience, the members of the audience itself. Lawyers in court must recognize only the judge and the "gentlemen of the jury." In a debate on the first draft for the League of Nations presided over by the Governor of Massachusetts, Senator Lodge's salutation was "Your Excellency, Ladies and Gentlemen, My Fellow Americans." The last was added unquestionably because patriotic feeling was so strong at the time that reference to our nationality was a decidedly fitting compliment, and also perhaps, because the speaker realized that his audience might be slightly prejudiced against the view he was going to advance in criticizing the League Covenant. At times a formal salutation becomes quite long to include all to whom recognition is due. At a university commencement a speaker might begin: "Mr. Chancellor, Members of the Board of Trustees, Gentlemen of the Faculty, Candidates for Degrees, Ladies and Gentlemen."

Other salutations are Your Honor, Mr. President, Mr. Speaker, Madame President, Madame Chairman, Mr. Chairman, Mr. Stevenson, Sir, Mr. Toastmaster, Mr. Moderator, Honorable Judges, Ladies, Gentlemen, Fellow Citizens, Classmates, Fellow Workers, Gentlemen of the Senate, Gentlemen of the Congress, Plenipotentiaries of the German Empire, My Lord Mayor and Citizens of London; Mr. Mayor, Mr. Secretary, Admiral Fletcher and Gentlemen of the Fleet; Mr. Grand Master, Governor McMillan, Mr. Mayor, My Brothers, Men and Women of Tennessee.

The most important thing about the salutation is that it should never be omitted. To begin to speak without having first recognized some presiding officer and the audience stamps one immediately as thoughtless, unpractised, or worse still—discourteous.

Having observed the propriety of the salutation the speaker should make a short pause before he proceeds to the introduction of his speech proper.

Length of the Introduction. There was a time when long elaborate introductions were the rule, and textbooks explained in detail how to develop them. The main assumption seems to have been that the farther away from his topic the speaker began, the longer and more indirect the route by which he approached it, the more sudden and surprising the start with which it was disclosed to the audience, the better the speech. Such views are no longer held. One of the criticisms of the speeches of the English statesman, Burke, is that instead of coming at once to the important matter under consideration—and all his speeches were upon paramount issues—he displayed his rhetorical skill and literary ability before men impatient to finish discussion and provide for action by casting their votes. If a student will read the beginning of Burke's famous *Speech on Conciliation* he will readily understand the force of this remark, for instead of bringing forward the all-important topic of arranging for colonial adjustment Burke uses hundreds of words upon the "flight of a bill for ever," his own pretended superstitiousness and belief in omens. So strong is the recognition of the opposite practice today that it is at times asserted that speeches should dispense with introductions longer than a single sentence.

Purpose of the Introduction. So far as the material of the speech is concerned the introduction has but one purpose—to bring the topic of the succeeding remarks clearly and arrestingly before the audience. It should be clearly done, so that there shall be no misunderstanding from the beginning. It should be arrestingly done, so that the attention shall be aroused and held from this announcement even until the end. A man should not declare that he is going to explain the manufacture of paper-cutters, and then later proceed to describe the making of those frames into which rolls of wrapping paper are fitted underneath a long cutting blade, because to most people the expression "paper-cutters" means dull-edged, ornamental knives for desks and library tables. His introduction would not be clear. On the other hand if a minister were to state plainly that he was going to speak on the truth that "it is more blessed to give than to receive" his congregation might turn its attention to its own affairs at once because the topic promises no novelty. But if he declares that he is going to make a defense of selfishness he would surely startle his hearers into attention, so that he could go on to describe the personal satisfaction and peace of mind which comes to the doers of good deeds. A speaker could arrest attention by stating that he intended to prove the immorality of the principle that "honesty is the best policy," if he proceeded to plead for that virtue not as a repaying *policy* but as an innate guiding principle of right, no matter what the consequences. In humorous, half-jesting, ironical material, of course, clearness may be justifiably sacrificed to preserving interest. The introduction may state the exact opposite of the real topic.

When nothing else except the material of the introduction need be considered, it should be short. Even in momentous matters this is true. Notice the brevity of the subjoined introduction of a speech upon a deeply moving subject.

> Gentlemen of the Congress:
>
> The Imperial German Government on the 31st day of January announced to this Government and to the Governments of the other neutral nations that on and after the 1st day of February, the present month, it would adopt a policy with regard to the use of submarines against all shipping seeking to pass through certain designated areas of the high seas, to which it is clearly my duty to call your attention.
>
> WOODROW WILSON, 1917

The following, though much longer, aims to do the same thing—to announce the topic of the speech clearly. Notice that in order to emphasize this endeavor to secure clearness the speaker declares that he has repeatedly tried to state his position in plain English. He then makes clear that he is not opposed to *a* League of Nations; he is merely opposed to the terms already submitted for the one about to be formed. This position he makes quite clear in the last sentence here quoted.

> Your Excellency, Ladies and Gentlemen, My Fellow Americans:
>
> I am largely indebted to President Lowell for this opportunity to address this great audience. He and I are friends of many years, both Republicans. He is the president of our great university, one of the most important and influential places in the United States. He is also an eminent student and historian of politics and government. He and I may differ as to methods in this great question now before the people, but I am sure that in regard to the security of the peace of the world and the welfare of the United States we do not differ in purposes.

I am going to say a single word, if you will permit me, as to my own position. I have tried to state it over and over again. I thought I had stated it in plain English. But there are those who find in misrepresentation a convenient weapon for controversy, and there are others, most excellent people, who perhaps have not seen what I have said and who possibly have misunderstood me. It has been said that I am against any League of Nations. I am not; far from it. I am anxious to have the nations, the free nations of the world, united in a league, as we call it, a society, as the French call it, but united, to do all that can be done to secure the future peace of the world and to bring about a general disarmament.

SENATOR HENRY CABOT LODGE in a debate in Boston, 1919

The Introduction and the Audience. When we turn from the material of the introduction or the speech we naturally consider the audience. Just as the salutations already listed in this chapter indicate how careful speakers are in adapting their very first words to the special demands of recognition for a single audience, so a study of introductions to speeches which have been delivered will support the same principle. A speech is made to affect a single audience, therefore it must be fitted as closely as possible to that audience in order to be effective. A city official invited to a neighborhood gathering to instruct citizens in the method of securing a children's playground in that district is not only wasting time but insulting the brains and dispositions of his listeners if he drawls off a long introduction showing the value of public playgrounds in a crowded city. His presence before that group of people proves that they accept all he can tell them on that topic. He is guilty of making a bad introduction which seriously impairs the value of anything he may say later concerning how this part of the city can induce the municipal government to set aside enough money to provide the open space and the apparatus. Yet this speech was made in a large American city by an expert on playgrounds.

People remembered more vividly his wrong kind of opening remarks than they did his advice concerning a method of procedure.

Effect of the Introduction upon the Audience. Many centuries ago a famous and successful Roman orator stipulated the purpose of an introduction with respect to the audience. Cicero stated that an introduction should render its hearers "*benevolos, attentos, dociles*"; that is, kindly disposed towards the speaker himself, attentive to his remarks, and willing to be instructed by his explanations or arguments. Not everyone has a pleasing personality but he can strive to acquire one. He can, perhaps, not add many attributes to offset those nature has given him, but he can always reduce, eradicate, or change those which interfere with his reception by others. Education and training will work wonders for people who are not blessed with that elusive quality, charm, or that winner of consideration, impressiveness. Self-examination, self-restraint, self-development, are prime elements in such a process. Great men have not been beyond criticism for such qualities. Great men have recognized their value and striven to rid themselves of hindrances and replace them by helps.

Every reader is familiar with Benjamin Franklin's account of his own method as related in his *Autobiography*, yet it will bear quotation here to illustrate this point:

> While I was intent on improving my language, I met with an English Grammar (I think it was Greenwood's), at the end of which there were two little sketches of the arts of rhetoric and logic, the latter "finishing with a specimen of a dispute in the Socratic method; and soon after I procured Xenophon's Memorable Things of Socrates, wherein there are many instances of the same method. I was charmed with it, adopted it, dropt my abrupt contradiction and positive argumentation, and put on the humble inquirer and doubter.... I found this method safest for myself and very embarrassing to those against whom I used it; therefore I took a delight in it, practised it continually, and grew very artful and expert in drawing people, even of superior knowledge, into concessions, the consequences of which they did not foresee, entangling them in difficulties out of which they could not extricate themselves, and so obtaining victories that neither myself nor my cause always deserved. I continued this method some few years, but gradually left it, retaining only the habit of expressing myself in terms of modest

diffidence; never using, when I advanced anything that may possibly be disputed, the words *Certainly, Undoubtedly*, or any others that give the air of positiveness to an opinion; but rather say, I conceive or apprehend a thing to be so and so; it appears to me, or *I should think it so or so*, for such and such reasons; or *I imagine it to be so*; or *it is so if I am not mistaken*. This habit, I believe, has been of great advantage to me when I have had occasion to inculcate my opinions, and persuade men into measures that I have been from time to time engaged in promoting; and as the chief ends of conversation are to *inform* or to be *informed*, to *please* or to *persuade*, I wish well-meaning, sensible men would not lessen their power of doing good by a positive, assuming manner, that seldom fails to disgust, tends to create opposition, and to defeat everyone of those purposes for which speech was given to us, to wit, giving or receiving information or pleasure. For if you would inform, a positive and dogmatical manner in advancing your sentiments may provoke contradiction and prevent a candid attention. If you wish information and improvement from the knowledge of others, and yet at the same time express yourself as firmly fixed in your present opinions, modest, sensible men who do not love disputation will probably leave you undisturbed in the possession of your error. And by such a manner you can seldom hope to recommend yourself in *pleasing* your hearers, or to persuade those whose concurrence you desire. Pope says, judiciously:

> "Men should be taught as if you taught them not,
> And things unknown propos'd as things forgot;"

farther recommending to us

> "To speak, tho' sure, with seeming diffidence."

Of course an audience must be induced to listen. The obligation is always with the speaker. He is appealing for consideration, he wants to affect the hearers, therefore he must have at his command all the resources of securing their respectful attention. He must be able to employ all the legitimate means of winning their attention. A good speaker will not stoop to use any tricks or devices that are not legitimate. A trick, even when it is successful, is still nothing but a trick, and though it secure the temporary attention of the lower orders of intellect it can never hold the better minds of an audience. Surprises, false alarms, spectacular appeals, may find their defenders. One widely reputed United States lawyer in speaking before audiences of young people used to advance theatrically to the edge of the stage, and, then, pointing an accusing finger at one part of the audience, declare in loud ringing tones, "You're a sneak!" It is questionable whether any attempt at arousing interest could justify such a brusque approach. Only in broadly comic or genuinely humorous addresses can it be said that the end justifies the means.

When the audience has been induced to listen, the rest should be easy for the good speaker. Then comes into action his skill at explanation, his ability to reason and convince, to persuade and sway, which is the speaker's peculiar art. If they will listen to him, he should be able to instruct them. The introduction must, so far as this last is concerned, clear the way for the remainder of the speech. The methods by which such instruction, reasoning, and persuasion are effected best will be treated later in this book.

Having covered the preceding explanation of the aims and forms of introductions, let us look at a few which have been delivered by regularly practising speech-makers before groups of men whose interest, concern, and business it was to listen. All men who speak frequently are extremely uneven in their quality and just as irregular in their success. One of the best instances of this unevenness and irregularity was Edmund Burke, whose career and practice are bound to afford food for thought and discussion to every student of the power and value of the spoken word. Some of Burke's speeches are models for imitation and study, others are warnings for avoidance. At one time when he felt personally disturbed by the actions of the House of Commons, because he as a member of the minority could not affect the voting, he began a speech exactly as no man should under any circumstances. No man in a deliberative assembly can be excused for losing control of himself. Yet Burke opened his remarks with these plain words.

"Mr. Speaker! I rise under some embarrassment occasioned by a feeling of delicacy toward one-half of the House, and of sovereign contempt for the other half."

This is childish, of course. A man may not infrequently be forced by circumstances to speak before an audience whose sentiments, opinions, prejudices, all place them in a position antagonistic to his own. How shall he make them well-disposed, attentive, willing to be instructed? The situation is not likely to surround a beginning speaker, but men in affairs, in business, in courts, must be prepared for such circumstances. One of the most striking instances of a man who attempted to speak before an antagonistic group and yet by sheer power of his art and language ended by winning them to his own party is in Shakespeare's *Julius Caesar* when Mark Antony speaks over his dead friend's body. Brutus allows it, but insists on speaking to the people first that he may explain why he and his fellow conspirators assassinated the great leader. It was a mistake to allow a person from the opposite party to have the last word before the populace, but that is not the point just here. Brutus is able to explain why a group of noble Romans felt that for the safety of the state and its inhabitants, they had to kill the rising favorite who would soon as King rule them all. When he ceases speaking, the citizens approve the killing. Mark Antony perceives that, so at the beginning of his speech he seems to agree with the people. Caesar was his friend, yet Brutus says he was ambitious, and Brutus is an honorable man. Thus the skilful orator makes the populace well-disposed towards him, then attentive.

Having secured those things he proceeds slowly and unobtrusively to instruct them. It takes only a few lines until he has made them believe all he wants them to; before the end of his oration he has them crying out upon the murderers of their beloved Caesar, for whose lives they now thirst. Yet only ten minutes earlier they were loudly acclaiming them as deliverers of their country. The entire scene should be analyzed carefully by the student. It is the second scene of the third act of the play.

In actual life a man would hardly have to go so far as seemingly to agree with such opposite sentiments as expressed in this situation from a stage tragedy. It is general knowledge that during the early years of the American Civil War England sympathized with the southern states, mainly because the effective blockade maintained by the North prevented raw cotton from reaching the British mills. Henry Ward Beecher attempted to present the union cause to the English in a series of addresses throughout the country. When he appeared upon the platform in Liverpool the audience broke out into a riot of noise which effectively drowned all his words for minutes. The speaker waited until he could get in a phrase. Finally he was allowed to deliver a few sentences. By his patience, his appeal to their English sense of fair play, and to a large degree by his tolerant sense of humor, he won their attention. His material, his power as a speaker did all the rest.

It is a matter of very little consequence to me, personally, whether I speak here tonight or not. [*Laughter and cheers.*] But one thing is very certain, if you do permit me to speak here tonight, you will hear very plain talking. [*Applause and hisses.*] You will not find me to be a man that dared to speak about Great Britain three thousand miles off, and then is afraid to speak to Great Britain when he stands on her shores. [*Immense applause and hisses.*] And if I do not mistake the tone and temper of Englishmen they had rather have a man who opposes them in a manly way [*applause from all parts of the hall*] than a sneak that agrees with them in an unmanly way. [*Applause and "Bravo!"*] Now, if I can carry you with me by sound convictions, I shall be immensely glad [*applause*]; but if I cannot carry you with me by facts and sound arguments, I do not wish you to go with me at all; and all that I ask is simply fair play. [*Applause, and a voice: "You shall have it too.".*]

Those of you who are kind enough to wish to favor my speaking —and you will observe that my voice is slightly husky, from having spoken almost every night in succession for some time past—those who wish to hear me will do me the kindness simply to sit still and to keep still; and I and my friends the Secessionists will make the noise. [*Laughter.*]

HENRY WARD BEECHER, in speech at Liverpool, 1863

The beginning of one of Daniel Webster's famous speeches was a triumph of the deliverer's recognition of the mood of an audience. In the Senate in 1830 feeling had been running high over a resolution concerning public lands. Innocent enough in its appearance, this resolution really covered an attempt at the extension of the slavery territory. Both North and South watched the progress of the debate upon this topic with almost held breath. Hayne of South Carolina had spoken upon it during two days when Webster rose to reply to him. The Senate galleries were packed, the members themselves were stirred up to the highest pitch of keen intensity. Nearly the entire effect of Webster's statement and argument for the North depended upon the effect he could make upon the Senators at the very opening of his speech.

Webster began in a low voice, with a calm manner, to speak very slowly. In a second he had soothed the emotional tension, set all the hearers quite at ease, and by the time the Secretary had read the resolution asked by Webster, he had them in complete control. His task was to make them attentive, but more especially, ready to be instructed.

> Mr. President: When the mariner has been tossed for many days in thick weather and on an unknown sea, he naturally avails himself of the first pause in the storm, the earliest glance of the sun, to take his latitude and ascertain how far the elements have driven him from his true course. Let us imitate this prudence; and, before we float farther on the waves of this debate, refer to the point from which we departed, that we may, at least, be able to conjecture where we now are. I ask for the reading of the resolution before the Senate.

DANIEL WEBSTER: Reply to Hayne, 1830

Linking the Introduction to Preceding Speeches. So many speeches are replies to preceding addresses that many introductions adapt themselves to their audiences by touching upon such utterances. In debates, in pleas in court, in deliberative assemblies, this is more usually the circumstance than not. The following illustrates how courteously this may be done, even when it serves merely to make all the clearer the present speaker's position. In moments of tensest feeling great speakers skilfully move from any one position or attitude to another as Patrick Henry did. While you are regarding these paragraphs as an example of introduction do not overlook their vocabulary and sentences.

> Mr. President: No man thinks more highly than I do of the patriotism, as well as abilities, of the very worthy gentlemen who have just addressed the house. But different men often see the same subject in different lights; and, therefore, I hope it will not be thought disrespectful to those gentlemen, if, entertaining as I do opinions of a character very opposite to theirs, I shall speak forth my sentiments freely, and without reserve. This is no

time for ceremony. The question before the house is one of awful moment to the country. For my own part, I consider it as nothing less than a question of freedom or slavery. And in proportion to the magnitude of the subject ought to be the freedom of the debate. It is only in this way that we can hope to arrive at truth, and fulfill the great responsibility which we hold to God and our country. Should I keep back my opinions at such a time, through fear of giving offense, I should consider myself as guilty of treason towards my country, and of an act of disloyalty toward the Majesty of Heaven, which I revere above all earthly things.

Mr. President, it is natural to man to indulge in the illusions of hope. We are apt to shut our eyes against a painful truth, and listen to the song of that Siren till she transforms us into beasts. Is this the part of wise men, engaged in a great and arduous struggle for liberty? Are we disposed to be of the number of those who having eyes see not, and having ears hear not, the things which so nearly concern their temporal salvation? For my part, whatever anguish of spirit it may cost, I am willing to know the whole truth; to know the worst and to provide for it.

PATRICK HENRY in the Virginia Convention, 1775

Difficulties of Introductions. People who are scheduled to make speeches are heard to declare that they know exactly what they want to say but they do not know how to begin. Another way they have of expressing this is that they do not know how to bring their material before their hearers. Undoubtedly the most difficult parts of speeches are the beginnings and conclusions. In Chapter II one of the methods of preparing for delivery recognized this difference by recording that one way is to memorize the beginning and ending, the opening and closing sentences. Practised speakers are more likely not to fix too rigidly in their minds any set way for starting to speak. They realize that a too carefully prepared opening will smack of the study. The conditions under which the speech is actually delivered may differ so widely from the anticipated surroundings that a speaker should be able to readjust his ideas instantly, seize upon any detail of feeling, remark, action, which will help him into closer communication with his audience. Many practised speakers, therefore, have at their wits' ends a dozen different manners, so that their appearance may fit in best with the circumstances, and their remarks have that air of easy spontaneity which the best speaking should have. Thus, sometimes, the exactly opposite advice of the method described above and in Chapter II is given. A speaker will prepare carefully his speech proper, but leave to circumstances the suggestion of the beginning he will use. This does not mean that he will not be prepared—it means that he will be all the more richly furnished with expedients. A speaker should carefully think over all the possibilities under which his speech will be brought forward, then prepare the best introduction to suit each set.

Spirit of the Introduction. The combination of circumstances and material will determine what we shall call the spirit of the introduction. In what spirit is the introduction treated? There are as many different treatments as there are human feelings and sentiments. The spirit may be serious, informative, dignified, scoffing, argumentative, conversational, startling, humorous, ironic. The student should lengthen this list by adding as many other adjectives as he can.

The serious treatment is always effective when it is suitable. There is a conviction of earnestness and sincerity about the speech of a man who takes his subject seriously. Without arousing opposition by too great a claim of importance for his topic he does impress its significance upon listeners. This seriousness must be justified by the occasion. It must not be an attempt to bolster up weakness of ideas or commonplaceness of expression. It must be straightforward, manly, womanly. Notice the excellent effect of the following which illustrates this kind of treatment.

> MAY IT PLEASE YOUR HONOR: I was desired by one of the court to look into the books, and consider the question now before them concerning Writs of Assistance. I have accordingly considered it, and appear not only in obedience to your order, but likewise in behalf of the inhabitants of this town, who have presented another petition, and out of regard to the liberties of the subject. And I take this opportunity to declare, that whether under a fee or not (for in such a cause as this I despise a fee) I will to my dying day oppose with all the powers and faculties God has

given me, all such instruments of slavery on the one hand and villainy on the other, as this Writ of Assistance is.

It appears to me the worst instrument of arbitrary power, the most destructive of English liberty and the fundamental principles of law, that ever was found in an English law-book.

JAMES OTIS: On Writs of Assistance, 1761

Informative and argumentative introductions are quite usual. They abound in legislative bodies, business organizations, and courts of law. Having definite purposes to attain they move forward as directly and clearly as they can. In such appearances a speaker should know how to lead to his topic quickly, clearly, convincingly. Introductions should be reduced to a minimum because time is valuable. Ideas count; mere talk is worthless.

Attempts at humorous speeches are only too often the saddest exhibitions of life. The mere recital of "funny stories" in succession is in no sense speech-making, although hundreds of misguided individuals act as though they think so. Nor is a good introduction the one that begins with a comic incident supposedly with a point pat to the occasion or topic, yet so often miles wide of both. The funny story which misses its mark is a boomerang. Even the apparently "sure-fire" one may deliver a disturbing kick to its perpetrator. The grave danger is the "o'er done or come tardy off" of Hamlet's advice to the players. Humor must be distinctly marked off from the merely comic or witty, and clearly recognized as a wonderful gift bestowed on not too many mortals in this world. The scoffing, ironic introduction may depend upon wit and cleverness born in the head; the humorous introduction depends upon a sympathetic instinct treasured in the heart. Look back at the remarks made by Beecher to his turbulent disturbers in Liverpool. Did he help his cause by his genial appreciation of their sentiments?

The student should study several introductions to speeches in the light of all the preceding discussions so that he may be able to prepare his own and judge them intelligently. Printed speeches will provide material for study, but better still are delivered remarks. If the student can hear the speech, then see it in print, so much the better, for he can then recall the effect in sound of the phrases.

Preparing and Delivering Introductions. Actual practice in preparation and delivery of introductions should follow. These should be delivered before the class and should proceed no farther than the adequate introduction to the hearers of the topic of the speech. They need not be so fragmentary as to occupy only three seconds. By supposing them to be beginnings of speeches from six to fifteen minutes long these remarks may easily last from one to two minutes.

Aside from the method of its delivery—pose, voice, speed, vocabulary, sentences—each introduction should be judged as an actual introduction to a real speech. Each speaker should keep in mind these questions to apply during his preparation. Each listener should apply them as he hears the introduction delivered.

Is the topic introduced gracefully?
Is it introduced clearly?
Is the introduction too long?
Does it begin too far away from the topic?
Is it interesting?
Has it any defects of material?
Has it any faults of manner?
Can any of it be omitted?
Do you want to hear the entire speech?
Can you anticipate the material?
Is it adapted to its audience?
Is it above their heads?
Is it beneath their intelligences?

Topics for these exercises in delivering introductions should be furnished by the interests, opinions, ideas, experiences, ambitions of the students themselves. Too many beginning speakers cause endless worry for themselves, lower the quality of their speeches, bore their listeners, by "hunting" for things to talk about, when near at hand in themselves and their activities lie the very best things to discuss. The over-modest feeling some people have that they know nothing to talk about is usually a false impression. In Elizabethan England a young poet, Sir Phillip Sidney, decided to try to tell his sweetheart how much he loved her. So he "sought fit words, studying inventions fine, turning others' leaves, to see if thence would flow, some fresh and fruitful showers upon my sunburnt brain." But "words came halting forth" until he bit his truant pen and almost beat himself for spite. Then said the Muse to him, "Fool, look in thy heart and write." And without that first word, this is the advice that should be given to all speakers. "Look in your heart, mind, life, experiences, ideas, ideals, interests, enthusiasms, and from them draw the material of your speeches—*yours* because no one else could make that speech, so essentially and peculiarly is it your own."

The following may serve as suggestions of the kind of topic to choose and the various methods of approaching it. They are merely hints, for each student must adapt his own method and material.

EXERCISES

1. By a rapid historical survey introduce the discussion that women will be allowed to vote in the United States.

2. By a historical survey introduce the topic that war will cease upon the earth.

3. Using the same method introduce the opposite.

4. Using some history introduce the topic that equality for all men is approaching.

5. Using the same method introduce the opposite.

6. Starting with the amount used introduce an explanation of the manufacture of cotton goods. Any other manufactured article may be used.

7. Starting with an incident to illustrate its novelty, or speed, or convenience, or unusualness, lead up to the description or explanation of some mechanical contrivance.

Dictaphone
Adding machine
Comptometer
Wireless telegraph
Knitting machine
Moving picture camera

Moving picture machine
Self-starter
Egg boiler
Newspaper printing press
Power churn
Bottle-making machine
Voting machine
Storm in a play
Pneumatic tube
Periscope, etc.

8. Describe some finished product (as a cup of tea, a copper cent) as introduction to an explanation of its various processes of development.

9. Start with the opinion that reading should produce pleasure to introduce a recommendation of a book.

10. Start with the opinion that reading should impart information to introduce a recommendation of a book.

11. Start with the money return a business or profession offers to introduce a discussion advising a person to follow it or not.

12. Beginning with the recent war lead up to the topic that military training should be a part of all regular education.

13. Beginning from the same point introduce the opposite.

14. Beginning with an item—or a fictitious item—from a newspaper recounting an accident lead up to workmen's compensation laws, or preventive protective measures in factories, or some similar topic.

15. Using a personal or known experience introduce some topic dealing with the survival of superstitions.

16. Choosing your own material and treatment introduce some theme related to the government, or betterment of your community.

17. Introduce a topic dealing with the future policy of your city, county, state, or nation.

18. Lead up to the statement of a change you would like to recommend strongly for your school.

19. In as interesting a manner as possible lead up to a statement of the business or profession you would like to follow.

20. Introduce a speech in which you intend to condemn something, by dealing with your introductory material ironically.

21. Imagine that you are presiding at a meeting of some club, society, or organization which has been called to discuss a definite topic. Choose the topic for discussion and deliver the speech bringing it before the session.

22. You have received a letter from a member of some organization who suggests that a society to which you belong join with it in some kind of contest or undertaking. Present the suggestion to your society.

23. You believe that soma memorial to the memory of some person should be established in your school, lodge, church, club. Introduce the subject to a group of members so that they may discuss it intelligently.

24. Introduce some topic to the class, but so phrase your material that the announcement of the topic will be a complete surprise to the members. Try to lead them away from the topic, yet so word your remarks that later they will realize that everything you said applies exactly to the topic you introduce.

25. Lead up to the recital of some mystery, or ghostly adventure.

26. Lead up to these facts. "For each 10,000 American-born workmen in a steel plant in eight years, 21 were killed; and for each non-English speaking foreign born, 26 were killed. Non-English speaking show 65 permanently disabled as compared with 28 who spoke English. Of temporarily disabled only 856 spoke English as compared with 2035 who did not."

27. Introduce the topic: Training in public speaking is valuable for all men and women.

28. In a genial manner suitable to the season's feelings introduce some statement concerning New Year's resolutions.

29. Frame some statement concerning aviation. Introduce it.

30. Introduce topics or statements related to the following:

The eight-hour day.
The principles of Socialism.
Legitimate methods of conducting strikes.
Extending the Monroe Doctrine.
Studying the classics, or modern languages.
Private fortunes.
College education for girls.
Direct presidential vote.
A good magazine.
Some great woman.
Sensible amusements.
Fashions.
Agriculture.
Business practice.
Minimum wages.
Equal pay for men and women.

CHAPTER V

CONCLUDING THE SPEECH

Preparing the Conclusion. No architect would attempt to plan a building unless he knew the purpose for which it was to be used. No writer of a story would start to put down words until he knew exactly how his story was to end. He must plan to bring about a certain conclusion. The hero and heroine must be united in marriage. The scheming villain must be brought to justice. Or if he scorn the usual ending of the "lived happily ever after" kind of fiction, he can plan to kill his hero and heroine, or both; or he can decide for once that his story shall be more like real life than is usually the case, and have wickedness triumph over virtue. Whatever he elects to do at the conclusion of his story, whether it be long or short, the principle of his planning is the same—he must know what he is going to do and adequately prepare for it during the course of, previous events.

One other thing every writer must secure. The ending of a book must be the most interesting part of it. It must rise highest in interest. It must be surest of appeal. Otherwise the author runs the risk of not having people read his book through to its conclusion, and as every book is written in the hope and expectation that it will be read through, a book which fails to hold the attention of its readers defeats its own purpose.

The foregoing statements are self-evident but they are set down because their underlying principles can be transferred to a consideration of the preparation of conclusions for speeches.

Is a Conclusion Necessary? But before we use them let us ask whether all speeches require conclusions.

There are some people—thoughtless, if nothing worse—who habitually end letters by adding some such expression as "Having nothing more to say, I shall now close." Is there any sense in writing such a sentence? If the letter comes only so far and the signature follows, do not those items indicate that the writer has nothing more to say and is actually closing? Why then, when a speaker has said all he has to say, should he not simply stop and sit down? Will that not indicate quite clearly that he has finished his speech? What effect would such an ending have?

In the first place the speaker runs the risk of appearing at least discourteous, if not actually rude, to his audience. To fling his material at them, then to leave it so, would impress men and women much as the brusque exit from a group of people in a room would or the slamming of a door of an office.

In the second place the speaker runs the graver risk of not making clear and emphatic the purpose of his speech. He may have been quite plain and effective during the course of his explanation or argument but an audience hears a speech only once. Can he trust to their recollection of what he has tried to impress upon them? Will they carry away exactly what he wants them to retain? Has he made the main topics, the chief aim, stand out prominently enough? Can he merely stop speaking? These are quite important aspects of a grave responsibility.

In the third place—though this may be considered less important than the preceding—the speaker gives the impression that he has not actually "finished" his speech. No one cares for unfinished articles, whether they be dishes of food, pieces of furniture, poems, or speeches. Without unduly stressing the fact that a speech is a carefully organized and constructed product, it may be stated that it is always a profitable effort to try to round off your remarks. A good conclusion gives an impression of completeness, of an effective product. Audiences are delicately susceptible to these impressions.

Twenty-two centuries ago Aristotle, in criticizing Greek oratory, declared that the first purpose of the conclusion was to conciliate the audience in favor of the speaker. As human nature has not changed much in the ages since, the statement still holds true.

Speakers, then, should provide conclusions for all their speeches.

Although the entire matter of planning the speech belongs to a later chapter some facts concerning it as they relate to the conclusion must be set down here.

Relation of the Conclusion to the Speech. The conclusion should reflect the purpose of the speech. It should enforce the reason for the delivery of the speech. As it emphasizes the purpose of the speech it should be in the speaker's mind before he begins to plan the development of his remarks. It should be kept constantly in his mind as he delivers his material. A train from Chicago bound for New York is not allowed to turn off on all the switches it meets in its journey. A speaker who wants to secure from a jury a verdict for damages from a traction company does not discuss presidential candidates. He works towards his conclusion. A legislator who wants votes to pass a bill makes his conclusion and his speech conform to that purpose. In all likelihood, his conclusion plainly asks for the votes he has been proving that his fellow legislators should cast. A school principal pleading with boys to stop gambling knows that his conclusion is going to be a call for a showing of hands to pledge support of his recommendations. A labor agitator knows that his conclusion is going to be an appeal to a sense of class prejudice, so he speaks with that continually in mind. An efficiency expert in shop management knows that his conclusion is going to enforce the saving in damages for injury by accident if a scheme of safety devices be installed, so he speaks with that conclusion constantly in his mind. In court the prosecuting attorney tells in his introduction exactly what he intends to prove. His conclusion shows that he has proved what he announced.

One is tempted to say that the test of a good speech, a well-prepared speech, is its conclusion. How many times one hears a speaker floundering along trying to do something, rambling about, making no impression, not advancing a pace, and then later receives from the unfortunate the confession, "I wanted to stop but I didn't know how to do it." No conclusion had been prepared beforehand. It is quite as disturbing to hear a speaker pass beyond the place where he could have made a good conclusion. If he realizes this he slips into the state of the first speaker described in this paragraph. If he does not realize when he reaches a good conclusion he talks too long and weakens the effect by stopping on a lower plane than he has already reached. This fault corresponds to the story teller whose book drops in interest at the end. The son of a minister was asked whether his father's sermon the previous Sunday had-not had some good points in it. The boy replied, "Yes, three good points where he should have stopped."

Length of the Conclusion. It must not be inferred from anything here stated concerning the importance of the conclusion that it need be long. A good rule for the length of the conclusion is the same rule that applies to the length of the introduction. It should be just long enough to do best what it is intended to do. As in the case of the introduction, so for the conclusion, the shorter the better, if consistent with clearness and effect. If either introduction or conclusion must deliberately be reduced the conclusion will stand the most compression. A conclusion will frequently fail of its effect if it is so long that the audience anticipates its main points. It fails if it is so long that it adds nothing of clearness or emphasis to the speech itself. It will end by boring if it is too long for the importance of its material. It will often produce a deeper, more lasting impression by its very conciseness. Brevity is the soul of more than mere humor. A brief remark will cut deeper than a long involved sentence. The speaker who had shown that the recent great war fails unless the reconstruction to be accomplished is worthy needed no more involved conclusion than the statement, "It is what we do tomorrow that will justify what we did yesterday."

Coupled with this matter of effect is the length of the speech itself. Short speeches are likely to require only short conclusions. Long speeches more naturally require longer conclusions.

Consider the following conclusions. Comment upon them. It would be interesting to try to decide the length of the speeches from which they are taken, then look at the originals, all of which are easily procurable at libraries.

> That is in substance my theory of what our foreign policy should
> be. Let us not boast, not insult any one, but make up our minds
> coolly what it is necesary to say, say it, and then stand to it,
> whatever the consequences may be.
>
> Theodore Roosevelt at Waukesha, 1903

The foregoing is quite matter-of-fact. It contains no emotional appeal at all. Yet even a strong emotional feeling can be put into a short conclusion. From the date and the circumstances surrounding the next the reader can easily picture for himself the intense emotion of the audience which listened to these words from the leader of the free states against the South.

Neither let us be slandered from our duty by false accusations against us, nor frightened from it by menaces of destruction to the government, nor of dungeons to ourselves. Let us have faith that right makes might, and in that faith let us to the end dare to do our duty as we understand it.

ABRAHAM LINCOLN: *Cooper Union Speech*, 1860

While the student planning his own speech must determine exactly what he shall put into his conclusion—depending always upon his material and his purpose—there are a few general hints which will help him.

The Retrospective Conclusion. A conclusion may be entirely retrospective. This means merely that it may refer back to the remarks which have been delivered in the body of the speech. A speaker does this to emphasize something he has already discussed by pointing out to his audience that he wants them to remember that from what he has said. Conclusions of this kind usually have no emotional appeal. They are likely to be found in explanatory addresses, where the clearness of the exposition should make hearers accept it as true. If a man has proven a fact—as in a law court—he does not have to make an appeal to feeling to secure a verdict. Juries are supposed to decide on the facts alone. This kind of conclusion emphasizes, repeats, clarifies, enforces. The first of the following is a good illustration of one kind of conclusion which refers to the remarks made in the speech proper. Notice that it enforces the speaker's opinions by a calm explanation of his sincerity.

> I want you to think of what I have said, because it represents all of the sincerity and earnestness that I have, and I say to you here, from this platform, nothing that I have not already stated in effect, and nothing I would not say at a private table with any of the biggest corporation managers in the land.

THEODORE ROOSEVELT at Fitchburg, 1902

The next, while it is exactly the same kind in material, adds some elements of stronger feeling. Yet in the main it also enforces the speaker's opinion by a clear explanation of his action. From this conclusion alone we know exactly the material and purpose of the entire speech.

Sir, I will detain you no longer. There are some parts of this bill which I highly approve; there are others in which I should acquiesce; but those to which I have now stated my objections appear to me so destitute of all justice, so burdensome and so dangerous to that interest which has steadily enriched, gallantly defended, and proudly distinguished us, that nothing can prevail upon me to give it my support.

DANIEL WEBSTER: *The Tariff*, 1824

The Anticipatory Conclusion. Just as a conclusion may be retrospective, so it may be anticipatory. It may start from the position defined or explained or reached by the speech and look forward to what may happen, what must be done, what should be instituted, what should be changed, what votes should be cast, what punishment should be inflicted, what pardons granted. The student should make a list of all possible things in the future which could be anticipated in the conclusions of various speeches. If one will think of the purposes of most delivered speeches he will realize that this kind of conclusion is much more frequent than the previous kind as so many speeches anticipate future action or events. Dealing with entirely different topics the three following extracts illustrate this kind of conclusion. Washington was arguing against the formation of parties in the new nation, trying to avert the inevitable.

There is an opinion that parties in free countries are useful checks upon the administration of the government, and serve to keep alive the spirit of liberty. This within certain limits is probably true; and in governments of a monarchical cast, patriotism may look with indulgence if not with favor upon the spirit of party. But in those of the popular character, in governments purely elective, it is a spirit not to be encouraged. From their natural tendency it is certain there will always be enough of that spirit for every salutary purpose. And there being constant danger of excess, the effort ought to be by force of public opinion to mitigate and assuage it. A fire not to be quenched, it demands a uniform vigilance to prevent its bursting into a flame, lest, instead of warming, it should consume.

With the dignity and the calmness of the preceding, contrast the Biblical fervor of the next—the magnanimous program of the reuniter of a divided people.

> With malice toward none; with charity for all; with firmness in the right, as God gives us to see the right, let us strive on to finish the work we are in; to bind up the nation's wounds; to care for him who shall have borne the battle, and for his widow and his orphan—to do all which may achieve and cherish a just and lasting peace among ourselves, and with all nations.

Abraham Lincoln: *Second Inaugural*, 1865

In totally different circumstances the next conclusion was delivered, yet it bears the same aspect of anticipation. There is not a single hint in it of the material of the speech which preceded it, it takes no glance backward, it looks forward only. Its effectiveness comes from the element of leadership, that gesture of pointing the way for loyal Americans to follow.

> No nation as great as ours can expect to escape the penalty of greatness, for greatness does not come without trouble and labor. There are problems ahead of us at home and problems abroad, because such problems are incident to the working out of a great national career. We do not shrink from them. Scant is our patience with those who preach the gospel of craven weakness. No nation under the sun ever yet played a part worth playing if it feared its fate overmuch—if it did not have the courage to be great. We of America, we, the sons of a nation yet in the pride of its lusty youth, spurn the teachings of distrust, spurn the creed of failure and despair. We know that the future is ours if we have in us the manhood to grasp it, and we enter the new century girding our loins for the contest before us, rejoicing in the struggle, and resolute so to bear ourselves that the nation's future shall even surpass her glorious past.

Theodore Roosevelt at Philadelphia, 1902

Grave times always make men look into the future. All acts are judged and justified after they are performed. All progress depends upon this straining the vision into the darkness of the yet-to-be. Upon the eve of great struggles anticipation is always uppermost in men's minds. In the midst of the strife it is man's hope. In the next extract, only one sentence glances backward.

> For us there is but one choice. We have made it. Woe be to the man or group of men that seeks to stand in our way in this day of high resolution when every principle we hold dearest is to be vindicated and made secure for the salvation of the nations. We are ready to plead at the bar of history, and our flag shall wear a new luster. Once more we shall make good with our lives and fortunes the great faith to which we were born, and a new glory shall shine in the face of our people.
>
> WOODROW WILSON: *Flag Day Address*, 1917

Retrospective and Anticipatory Conclusion. While it does not occur so frequently as the two kinds just illustrated it is possible for a conclusion to be both retrospective and anticipatory—to look both backward and forward. The conclusion may enforce what the speech has declared or proved, then using this position as a safe starting point for a new departure, look forward and indicate what may follow or what should be done. The only danger in such an attempt is that the dual aspect may be difficult to make effective. Either one may neutralize the other. Still, a careful thinker and master of clear language may be able to carry an audience with him in such a treatment. The division in the conclusion between the backward glance and the forward vision need not be equal. Here again the effect to be made upon the audience, the purpose of the speech, must be the determining factor. Notice how the two are blended in the following conclusion from a much read commemorative oration.

> And now, friends and fellow-citizens, it is time to bring this discourse to a close.
>
> We have indulged in gratifying recollections of the past, in the prosperity and pleasures of the present, and in high hopes for the future. But let us remember that we have duties and obligations to perform, corresponding to the blessings which we enjoy. Let

us remember the trust, the sacred trust, attaching to the rich inheritance which we have received from our fathers. Let us feel our personal responsibility, to the full extent of our power and influence, for the preservation of the principles of civil and religious liberty. And let us remember that it is only religion, and morals, and knowledge, that can make men respectable, under any form of government....

DANIEL WEBSTER: *Completion of Bunker Hill Monument*, 1843

Conclusions are classified in general under three headings: 1. Recapitulation; 2. Summary; 3. Peroration.

The Recapitulation. The first of these—recapitulation—is exactly defined by the etymology of the word itself. Its root is Latin *caput*, head. So recapitulation means the repetition of the heads or main topics of a preceding discussion. Coming at the end of an important speech of some length, such a conclusion is invaluable. If the speaker has explained clearly or reasoned convincingly his audience will have been enlightened or convinced. Then at the end, to assure them they are justified in their knowledge or conviction, he repeats in easily remembered sequence the heads which he has treated in his extended remarks. It is as though he chose from his large assortment a small package which he does up neatly for his audience to carry away with them. Frequently, too, the recapitulation corresponds exactly to the plan as announced in the introduction and followed throughout the speech. This firmly impresses the main points upon the brains of the hearers.

A lawyer in court starts by announcing that he will prove a certain number of facts. After his plea is finished, in the conclusion of his speech, he recapitulates, showing that he has proved these things. A minister, a political candidate, a business man, a social worker—in fact, every speaker will find such a clear-cut listing an informative, convincing manner of constructing a conclusion. This extract shows a clear, direct, simple recapitulation.

> To recapitulate what has been said, we maintain, first, that the Constitution, by its grants to Congress and its prohibitions on the states, has sought to establish one uniform standard of value,

or medium of payment. Second, that, by like means, it has endeavored to provide for one uniform mode of discharging debts, when they are to be discharged without payment. Third, that these objects are connected, and that the first loses much of its importance, if the last, also, be not accomplished. Fourth, that, reading the grant to Congress and the prohibition on the States together, the inference is strong that the Constitution intended to confer an exclusive power to pass bankrupt laws on Congress. Fifth, that the prohibition in the tenth section reaches to all contracts, existing or future, in the same way that the other prohibition, in the same section, extends to all debts, existing or future. Sixth, that, upon any other construction, one great political object of the Constitution will fail of its accomplishment.

DANIEL WEBSTER: Ogden vs. Saunders, 1827

The Summary. The second kind—a summary—does somewhat the same thing that the recapitulation does, but it effects it in a different matter. Note that the recapitulation *repeats* the main headings of the speech; it usually uses the same or similar phrasing.

The summary does not do this. The summary condenses the entire material of the speech, so that it is presented to the audience in shortened, general statements, sufficient to recall to them what the speaker has already presented, without actually repeating his previous statements. This kind of conclusion is perhaps more usual than the preceding one. It is known by a variety of terms—summing up, resume, epitome, review, precis, condensation.

In the first of the subjoined illustrations notice that the words "possible modes" contain practically all the speech itself. So the four words at the end, "faction, corruption, anarchy, and despotism," hold a great deal of the latter part of the speech. These expressions do not repeat the heads of divisions; they condense long passages. The extract is a summary.

> I have thus presented all possible modes in which a government founded upon the will of an absolute majority will be modified; and have demonstrated that, in all its forms, whether in a

majority of the people, as in a mere democracy, or in a majority of their representatives, without a constitution, to be interpreted as the will of the majority, the result will be the same: two hostile interests will inevitably be created by the action of the government, to be followed by hostile legislation, and that by faction, corruption, anarchy, and despotism.

JOHN C. CALHOUN: *Speech on the Force Bill, 1833*

From the following pick out the expressions which summarize long passages of the preceding speech. Amplify them to indicate what they might cover.

I firmly believe in my countrymen, and therefore I believe that the chief thing necessary in order that they shall work together is that they shall know one another—that the Northerner shall know the Southerner, and the man of one occupation know the man of another occupation; the man who works in one walk of life know the man who works in another walk of life, so that we may realize that the things which divide us are superficial, are unimportant, and that we are, and must ever be, knit together into one indissoluble mass by our common American brotherhood.

THEODORE ROOSEVELT at Chattanooga, 1902

The Peroration. A peroration is a conclusion which—whatever may be its material and treatment—has an appeal to the feelings, to the emotions. It strives to move the audience to act, to arouse them to an expression of their wills, to stir them to deeds. It usually comes at the end of a speech of persuasion. It appeals to sentiments of right, justice, humanity, religion. It seldom merely concludes a speech; it looks forward to some such definite action as casting a vote, joining an organization or movement, contributing money, going out on strike, returning to work, pledging support, signing a petition.

These purposes suggest its material. It is usually a direct appeal, personal and collective, to all the hearers. Intense in feeling, tinged with emotion, it justifies itself by its sincerity and honesty alone. Its apparent success is not the measure of its merit. Too frequently an appeal to low prejudices, class sentiment and prejudice, base motives, mob instincts will carry a group of people in a certain direction with as little sense and reason as a flock of sheep display. Every student can cite a dozen instances of such unwarranted and unworthy responses to skilful perverted perorations. Answering to its emotional tone the style of a peroration is likely to rise above the usual, to become less simple, less direct. In this temptation for the speaker lies a second danger quite as grave as the one just indicated. In an attempt to wax eloquent he is likely to become grandiloquent, bombastic, ridiculous. Many an experienced speaker makes an unworthy exhibition of himself under such circumstances. One specimen of such nonsense will serve as a warning.

When the terms for the use of the Panama Canal were drawn up there arose a discussion as to certain kinds of ships which might pass through the canal free of tolls. A treaty with Great Britain prevented tolls-exemption for privately owned vessels. In a speech in Congress upon this topic one member delivered the following inflated and inconsequential peroration. Can any one with any sanity see any connection of the Revolutionary War, Jefferson, Valley Forge, with a plain understanding of such a business matter as charging tolls for the use of a waterway? To get the full effect of this piece of "stupendous folly"—to quote the speaker's own words— the student should declaim it aloud with as much attempt at oratorical effect as its author expended upon it.

Now, may the God of our fathers, who nerved 3,000,000 backwoods Americans to fling their gage of battle into the face of the mightiest monarch in the world, who guided the hand of Jefferson in writing the charter of liberty, who sustained Washington and his ragged and starving army amid the awful horrors of Valley Forge, and who gave them complete victory on the blood-stained heights of Yorktown, may He lead members to vote so as to prevent this stupendous folly—this unspeakable humiliation of the American republic.

When the circumstances are grave enough to justify impassioned language a good speaker need not fear its effect. If it be suitable, honest, and sincere, a peroration may be as emotional as human feelings dictate. So-called "flowery language" seldom is the medium of deep feeling. The strongest emotions may be expressed in the simplest terms. Notice how, in the three extracts here quoted, the feeling is more intense in each succeeding one. Analyze the style. Consider the words, the phrases, the sentences in length and structure. Explain the close relation of the circumstances and the speaker with the material and the style. What was the purpose of each?

> Sir, let it be to the honor of Congress that in these days of political strife and controversy, we have laid aside for once the sin that most easily besets us, and, with unanimity of counsel, and with singleness of heart and of purpose, have accomplished for our country one measure of unquestionable good.

DANIEL WEBSTER: *Uniform System of Bankruptcy*, 1840

Lord Chatham addressed the House of Lords in protest against the inhumanities of some of the early British efforts to suppress the American Revolution.

> I call upon that right reverend bench, those holy ministers of the Gospel, and pious pastors of our Church—I conjure them to join in the holy work, and vindicate the religion of their God. I appeal to the wisdom and law of this learned bench, to defend and support the justice of their country. I call upon the Bishops to interpose the unsullied sanctity of their lawn; upon the

learned Judges, to interpose their purity upon the honor of your Lordships, to reverence the dignity of your ancestors and to maintain your own. I call upon the spirit and humanity of my country, to vindicate the national character. I invoke the genius of the Constitution. From the tapestry that adorns these walls the immortal ancestor of this noble Lord frowns with indignation at the disgrace of his country....

I again call upon your Lordships, and the united powers of the state, to examine it thoroughly and decisively, and to stamp upon it an indelible stigma of the public abhorrence. And I again implore those holy prelates of our religion to do away with these iniquities from among us! Let them perform a lustration; let them purify this House, and this country, from this sin.

My Lords, I am old and weak, and at present unable to say more; but my feelings and indignation were too strong to have said less. I could not have slept this night in my bed, nor reposed my head on my pillow, without giving vent to my eternal abhorrence of such preposterous and enormous principles.

At about the same time the same circumstances evoked several famous speeches, one of which ended with this well-known peroration.

It is in vain, Sir, to extenuate the matter. Gentlemen may cry, Peace, Peace—but there is no peace. The war is actually begun! The next gale that sweeps from the North will bring to our ears the clash of resounding arms! Our brethren are already in the field! Why stand we here idle? What is it that gentlemen wish? What would they have? Is life so dear, or peace so sweet, as to be purchased at the price of chains and slavery? Forbid it, Almighty God! I know not what course others may take; but as for me, give me liberty or give me death!

PATRICK HENRY in the Virginia Convention, 1775

Preparing and Delivering Conclusions. Students cannot very well be asked to prepare and deliver conclusions to speeches which do not yet exist, so there is no way of devising conclusions until later. But students should report upon conclusions to speeches they have recently listened to, and explain to the class their opinions concerning their material, methods, treatment, delivery, effect. The following questions will help in judging and criticizing:

Was the conclusion too long?
Was it so short as to seem abrupt?
Did it impress the audience?
How could it have been improved?
Was it recapitulation, summary, peroration?
Was it retrospective, anticipatory, or both?
What was its relation to the main part of the speech?
Did it refer to the entire speech or only a portion?
What was its relation to the introduction?
Did the speech end where it began?
Did it end as it began?
Was the conclusion in bad taste?
What was its style?
What merits had it?
What defects?
What suggestions could you offer for its improvement?
With reference to the earlier parts of the speech, how was it delivered?

The following conclusions should be studied from all the angles suggested in this chapter and previous ones. An air of reality will be secured if they are memorized and spoken before the class.

EXERCISES

> 1. There are many qualities which we need alike in private citizen and in public man, but three above all—three for the lack of which no brilliancy and no genius can atone—and those three are courage, honesty, and common sense.
>
> THEODORE ROOSEVELT at Antietam, 1903

> 2. Poor Sprat has perished despite his splendid tomb in the Abbey. Johnson has only a cracked stone and a worn-out inscription (for the Hercules in St. Paul's is unrecognizable) but

he dwells where he would wish to dwell—in the loving memory of men.

AUGUSTINE BIRRELL: *Transmission of Dr. Johnson's Personality*, 1884

3. So, my fellow citizens, the reason I came away from Washington is that I sometimes get lonely down there. There are so many people in Washington who know things that are not so, and there are so few people who know anything about what the people of the United States are thinking about. I have to come away and get reminded of the rest of the country. I have to come away and talk to men who are up against the real thing and say to them, "I am with you if you are with me." And the only test of being with me is not to think about me personally at all, but merely to think of me as the expression for the time being of the power and dignity and hope of the United States.

WOODROW WILSON: *Speech to the American Federation of Labor*, 1917

4. But if, Sir Henry, in gratitude for this beautiful tribute which I have just paid you, you should feel tempted to reciprocate by taking my horses from my carriage and dragging me in triumph through the streets, I beg that you will restrain yourself for two reasons. The first reason is—I have no horses; the second is—I have no carriage.

SIMEON FORD: *Me and Sir Henry* (Irving), 1899

5. Literature has its permanent marks. It is a connected growth and its life history is unbroken. Masterpieces have never been produced by men who have had no masters. Reverence for good work is the foundation of literary character. The refusal to praise bad work or to imitate it is an author's professional chastity.

Good work is the most honorable and lasting thing in the world. Four elements enter into good work in literature:—

An original impulse—not necessarily a new idea, but a new sense of the value of an idea.

A first-hand study of the subject and material.

A patient, joyful, unsparing labor for the perfection of form.

A human aim—to cheer, console, purify, or ennoble the life of the people. Without this aim literature has never sent an arrow close to the mark.

It is only by good work that men of letters can justify their right to a place in the world. The father of Thomas Carlyle was a stone-mason, whose walls stood true and needed no rebuilding. Carlyle's prayer was: "Let me write my books as he built his houses."

HENRY VAN DYKE: *Books, Literature and the People*, 1900

6. All this, I know well enough, will sound wild and chimerical to the profane herd of those vulgar and mechanical politicians who have no place among us—a sort of people who think that nothing exists but what is gross and material; and who, therefore, far from being qualified to be directors of the great movement of empire, are unfit to turn a wheel in the machine. But to men truly initiated and rightly taught, these ruling and master principles, which in the opinion of such men as I have mentioned have no substantial existence, are in truth everything and all in all. Magnanimity in politics is not seldom the truest wisdom: and a great empire and little minds go ill together. If we are conscious of our station, and glow with zeal to fill our places as becomes our situation and ourselves, we ought to auspicate all our public proceedings on America with the old warning of the church, *Sursum corda!* We ought to elevate our minds to the greatness of that trust to which the order of Providence has called us. By adverting to the dignity of this high calling, our ancestors have turned a savage wilderness into a glorious empire; and have made the most extensive, and the only honorable conquests, not by destroying, but by promoting

the wealth, the number, the happiness of the human race. Let us get an American revenue as we have got an American empire. English privileges have made it all that it is; English privileges alone will make it all it can be.

In full confidence of this unalterable truth, I now (*quod felix faustumque sit!*) lay the first stone of the Temple of Peace; and I move you;—

That the colonies and plantations of Great Britain in North America, consisting of fourteen separate governments, and containing two millions and upwards of free inhabitants, have not had the liberty and privilege of electing and sending any knights and burgesses, or others, to represent them in the high court of Parliament.

EDMUND BURKE: Conciliation with America, 1775

7. Now, Mr. Speaker, having fully answered all the arguments of my opponents, I will retire to the cloak-room for a few moments, to receive the congratulations of admiring mends.

JOHN ALLEN in a speech in Congress

8. Relying then on the patronage of your good will, I advance with obedience to the work, ready to retire from it whenever you become sensible how much better choice it is in your power to make. And may that Infinite Power which rules the destinies of the universe lead our councils to what is best, and give them a favorable issue for your peace and prosperity.

THOMAS JEFFERSON, First Inaugural, 1801

9. My friends, this is wholly an unprepared speech. I did not expect to be called or to say a word when I came here. I supposed I was merely to do something toward raising a flag. I may, therefore, have said something indiscreet. But I have said nothing but what I am willing to live by, and, if it be the pleasure of Almighty God, to die by.

10. I have spoken plainly because this seems to me the time when it is most necessary to speak plainly, in order that all the world may know that even in the heat and ardor of the struggle and when our whole thought is of carrying the war through to its end we have not forgotten any ideal or principle for which the name of America has been held in honor among the nations and for which it has been our glory to contend in the great generations that went before us. A supreme moment of history has come. The eyes of the people have been opened and they see. The hand of God is laid upon the nations. He will show them favor, I devoutly believe, only if they rise to the clear heights of His own justice and mercy.

WOODROW WILSON in a speech to Congress, 1917

11. This is what I have to say—ponder it; something you will agree with, something you will disagree with; but think about it, if I am wrong, the sooner the wrong is exposed the better for me —this is what I have to say: God is bringing the nations together. We must establish courts of reason for the settlement of controversies between civilized nations. We must maintain a force sufficient to preserve law and order among barbaric nations; and we have small need of an army for any other purpose. We must follow the maintenance of law and the establishment of order and the foundations of civilization with the vitalizing forces that make for civilization. And we must constantly direct our purpose and our policies to the time when the whole world shall have become civilized; when men, families, communities, will yield to reason and to conscience. And then we will draw our sword Excalibur from its sheath and fling it out into the sea, rejoicing that it is gone forever.

LYMAN ABBOTT: *International Brotherhood*, 1899

12. I give you, gentlemen, in conclusion, this sentiment: "The Little Court-room at Geneva—where our royal mother England, and her proud though untitled daughter, alike bent their heads to

the majesty of Law and accepted Justice as a greater and better arbiter than Power."

WILLIAM M. EVARTS: *International Arbitration*, 1872

13. You recollect the old joke, I think it began with Preston of South Carolina, that Boston exported no articles of native growth but granite and ice. That was true then, but we have improved since, and to these exports we have added roses and cabbages. Mr. President, they are good roses, and good cabbages, and I assure you that the granite is excellent hard granite, and the ice is very cold ice.

EDWARD EVERETT HALE: *Boston*, 1880

14. Long live the Republic of Washington! Respected by mankind, beloved of all its sons, long may it be the asylum of the poor and oppressed of all lands and religions—long may it be the citadel of that liberty which writes beneath the Eagle's folded wings, "We will sell to no man, we will deny to no man, Right and Justice."

Long live the United States of America! Filled with the free, magnanimous spirit, crowned by the wisdom, blessed by the moderation, hovered over by the guardian angel of Washington's example; may they be ever worthy in all things to be defended by the blood of the brave who know the rights of man and shrink not from their assertion—may they be each a column, and altogether, under the Constitution, a perpetual Temple of Peace, unshadowed by a Caesar's palace, at whose altar may freely commune all who seek the union of Liberty and Brotherhood.

Long live our Country! Oh, long through the undying ages may it stand, far removed in fact as in space from the Old World's feuds and follies, alone in its grandeur and its glory, itself the immortal monument of Him whom Providence commissioned to teach man the power of Truth, and to prove to the nations that their Redeemer liveth."

15. When that great and generous soldier, U.S. Grant gave back to Lee, crushed, but ever glorious, the sword he had surrendered at Appomattox, that magnanimous deed said to the people of the South: "You are our brothers." But when the present ruler of our grand republic on awakening to the condition of war that confronted him, with his first commission placed the leader's sword in the hands of those gallant Confederate commanders, Joe Wheeler and Fitzhugh Lee, he wrote between the lines in living letters of everlasting light the words: "There is but one people of this Union, one flag alone for all."

The South, Mr. Toastmaster, will feel that her sons have been well given, that her blood has been well spilled, if that sentiment is to be indeed the true inspiration of our nation's future. God grant it may be as I believe it will.

Clare Howell: *Our Reunited Country*, 1898

16. Two years ago last autumn, we walked on the sea beach together, and with a strange and prophetic kind of poetry, he likened the scene to his own failing health, the falling leaves, the withered sea-weed, the dying grass upon the shore, and the ebbing tide that was fast receding from us. He told me that he felt prepared to go, for he had forgiven his enemies, and could even rejoice in their happiness. Surely this was a grand condition in which to step from this world across the threshold to the next!

Joseph Jefferson: *In Memory of Edwin Booth*, 1893

17. A public spirit so lofty is not confined to other lands. You are conscious of its stirrings in your soul. It calls you to courageous service, and I am here to bid you obey the call. Such patriotism may be yours. Let it be your parting vow that it shall be yours. Bolingbroke described a patriot king in England; I can imagine a patriot president in America. I can see him indeed the choice of a party, and called to administer the government when

sectional jealousy is fiercest and party passion most inflamed. I can imagine him seeing clearly what justice and humanity, the national law and the national welfare require him to do, and resolved to do it. I can imagine him patiently enduring not only the mad cry of party hate, the taunt of "recreant" and "traitor," of "renegade" and "coward," but what is harder to bear, the amazement, the doubt, the grief, the denunciation, of those as sincerely devoted as he to the common welfare. I can imagine him pushing firmly on, trusting the heart, the intelligence, the conscience of his countrymen, healing angry wounds, correcting misunderstandings, planting justice on surer foundations, and, whether his party rise or fall, lifting his country heavenward to a more perfect union, prosperity, and peace. This is the spirit of a patriotism that girds the commonwealth with the resistless splendor of the moral law—the invulnerable panoply of states, the celestial secret of a great nation and a happy people.

GEORGE WILLIAM CURTIS: *The Public Duty of Educated Men*,
1877

CHAPTER VI.

GETTING MATERIAL

The Material of Speeches. So far this book has dealt almost entirely with the manner of speaking. Now it comes to the relatively more important consideration of the material of speech. Necessary as it is that a speaker shall know how to speak, it is much more valuable that he shall know what to speak. We frequently hear it said of a speaker, "It wasn't what he said, it was the way he said it," indicating clearly that the striking aspect of the delivery was his manner; but even when this remark is explained it develops frequently that there was some value in the material, as well as some charm or surprise or novelty in the method of expression. In the last and closest analysis a speech is valuable for what it conveys to its hearers' minds, what it induces them to do, not what temporary effects of charm and entertainment it affords.

Persons of keen minds and cultivated understandings have come away from gatherings addressed by men famous as good speech-makers and confessed to something like the following: "I was held spellbound all the time he was talking, but for the life of me, I can't tell you one thing he said or one idea he impressed upon me." A student should judge speeches he hears with such things in mind, so that he can hold certain ones up as models, and discard others as "horrible examples."

It should be the rule that before a man attempts to speak he should have something to say. This is apparently not always the case. Many a man tries to say something when he simply has nothing at all to say. Recall the description of Gratiano's talk, quoted earlier in this book.

A speaker then must have material. He must get material. The clergyman knows that he must deliver about a hundred sermons a year. The lawyer knows he must go into court on certain days. The lecturer must instruct his various audiences. The business man must address executive boards, committees, conventions, customers. The student must address classes, societies. The beginner in speech training must seize every opportunity to talk. Certainly the natural reserve stock of ideas and illustrations will soon be exhausted, or it will grow so stale that it will be delivered ineffectively, or it will be unsuitable to every occasion. A celebrated Frenchman, called upon unexpectedly to speak, excused himself by declaring, "What is suitable to say I do not know, and what I know is not suitable."

Getting Material. There are three ways of getting material. The first is by observation, the second by interview, the third by reading.

Observation. The value of securing material by observation is apparent at first glance. That which you have experienced you know. That which you have seen with your own eyes you can report correctly. That which has happened to you you can relate with the aspect of absolute truth. That which you have done you can teach others to do. That which has touched you you can explain correctly. That which you know to be the fact is proof against all attack.

These are the apparent advantages of knowledge gained at first hand. The faculty of accurate observation is one of the most satisfying that can enter into a person's mental equipment. It can be trained, broadened, and made more and more accurate. In some trades and professions it is an indispensable part of one's everyday ability. The faculty may be easily developed by exercise and test for accuracy.

Everyone acknowledges the weight and significance of material gained by observation. In America especially we accord attention and regard to the reports and accounts made by men who have done things, the men who have experienced the adventures they relate. There is such a vividness, a reality, a conviction about these personal utterances that we must listen respectfully and applaud sincerely. Magazines and newspapers offer hundreds of such articles for avid readers. Hundreds of books each year are based upon such material.

With all its many advantages the field of observation is limited. Not every person can experience or see all he is interested in and wants to talk about. We must choose presidents but we cannot observe the candidates themselves and their careers. We must have opinions about the League of Nations, the Mexican situation, the radical labor movements, the changing taxes, but we cannot observe all phases of these absorbing topics. If we restrict speeches to only what we can observe we shall all be uttering merely trivial personalities based upon no general knowledge and related to none of the really important things in the universe.

Nor is it always true that the person who does a thing can report it clearly and accurately. Ask a woman or girl how she hemstitches a handkerchief, or a boy how he swims or throws a curve, and note the involved and inaccurate accounts. If you doubt this, explain one of these to the class. It is not easy to describe exactly what one has seen, mainly because people do not see accurately. People usually see what they want to see, what they are predisposed to see. Witnesses in court, testifying upon oath concerning an accident, usually produce as many different versions as there are pairs of eyes. Books upon psychology report many enlightening and amusing cases of this defect of accurate observation in people. [2]

[2] Good cases are related by Swift, E.J.: *Psychology and the Day's Work.*

The two negative aspects of material secured in this first manner—1, limited range of observation, 2, inaccuracy of observation—placed beside the advantages already listed will clearly indicate in what subjects and circumstances this method should be relied upon for securing material for speeches.

EXERCISES

1. Make a list of recent articles based upon observation which you have seen or read in newspapers and magazines.

2. With what kind of material does each deal?

3. Which article is best? Why?

4. List four topics upon which your observation has given you material which could be used in a speech.

5. What kind of speech? A speech for what purpose?

6. Consider and weigh the value of your material.

7. Why is it good?

8. What limits, or drawbacks has it?

9. What could be said against it from the other side?

Interview. If a person cannot himself experience or observe all he wants to use for material his first impulse will be to interview people who have had experience themselves. In this circumstance the speaker becomes the reporter of details of knowledge furnished by others. The value of this is apparent at once. Next to first-hand knowledge, second-hand knowledge will serve admirably.

Every newspaper and magazine in the world uses this method because its readers' first query, mental or expressed, of all its informative articles is "Is this true?" If the author is merely repeating the experience of an acknowledged expert in the field under discussion, the value of the interview cannot be questioned. In this case the resulting report is almost as good as the original testimony or statement of the man who knows.

The first requisite, therefore, of material gathered in such a manner is that it be reproduced exactly as first delivered. The man who told a woman that a critic had pronounced her singing "heavenly" had good intentions but he was not entirely accurate in changing to that nattering term the critic's actual adjective "unearthly." The frequency with which alleged statements published in the daily press are contradicted by the supposed utterers indicates how usual such misrepresentation is, though it may be honestly unintentional. The speaker before an audience must be scrupulously correct in quoting. This accuracy is not assured unless a stenographic transcript be taken at the time the information is given, or unless the person quoted reads the sentiments and statements credited to him and expresses his approval.

Signed statements, personal letters, printed records, photographs, certified copies, and other exhibits of all kinds are employed to substantiate material secured from interviews and offered in speeches. If you notice newspaper accounts of lectures, political speeches, legislative procedure, legal practice, you will soon become familiar with such usages as are described by the expressions, filing as part of the record, taking of a deposition in one city for use in a lawsuit in another, Exhibit A, photograph of an account book, statement made in the presence of a third party, as recorded by a dictaphone, etc.

The first danger in securing material by the personal interview is the natural error of misunderstanding. The second danger is the natural desire—not necessarily false, at that—to interpret to the user's benefit, the material so secured, or to the discredit of all views other than his own. It is so easy, so tempting, in making out a strong case for one's own opinions to omit the slight concession which may grant ever so little shade of right to other beliefs. Judicious manipulation of any material may degenerate into mere juggling for support. Quotations and reports, like statistics, can be made to prove anything, and the general intellectual distrust of mere numbers is cleverly summed up in the remark, "Figures can't lie, but liars can figure."

To have the material accepted as of any weight or value the person from whom it is secured must be recognized as an authority. He must be of such eminence in the field for which his statements are quoted as not only to be accepted by the speaker using his material but as unqualifiedly recognized by all the opponents of the speaker. His remarks must have the definiteness of the expert witness whose testimony in court carries so much weight. To secure due consideration, the speaker must make perfectly clear to his audience the position of his authority, his fitness to be quoted, his unquestioned knowledge, sincerity, and honesty.

Knowledge secured in this manner may be used with signal effect in a speech, either to supply all the material or to cover certain portions. If you listen to many speeches (and you should), notice how often a speaker introduces the result of his interviews—formal or merely conversational— with persons whose statement he is certain will impress his audience.

EXERCISES

1. Make a list of five topics of which you know so little that you would have to secure information by interviews.

2. Of these choose two, define your opinion or feeling in each, and tell to whom you could apply for material.

3. Choose one dealing with some topic of current interest in your locality; define your own opinion or feeling, and tell to whom you could apply for material.

4. Explain exactly why you name this person.

5. Prepare a set of questions to bring out material to support your position.

6. Prepare some questions to draw out material to dispose of other views.

7. Interview some person upon one of the foregoing topics or a different one, and in a speech present this material before the class.

8. In general discussion comment on the authorities reported and the material presented.

Reading. The best way and the method most employed for gathering material is reading. Every user of material in speeches must depend upon his reading for the greatest amount of his knowledge. The old expression "reading law" shows how most legal students secured the information upon which their later practice was based. Nearly all real study of any kind depends upon wide and careful reading.

Reading, in the sense here used, differs widely from the entertaining perusal of current magazines, or the superficial skimming through short stories or novels. Reading for material is done with a more serious purpose than merely killing time, and is regulated according to certain methods which have been shown to produce the best results for the effort and time expended.

The speaker reads for the single purpose of securing material to serve his need in delivered remarks. He has a definite aim. He must know how to serve that end. Not everyone who can follow words upon a printed page can read in this sense. He must be able to read, understand, select, and retain. The direction is heard in some churches to "read, mark, learn, and inwardly digest." This is a picturesque phrasing of the same principles.

You must know how to read. Have you often in your way through a book suddenly realized at the bottom of a page that you haven't the slightest recollection of what your eye has been over? You may have felt this same way after finishing a chapter. People often read poetry in this manner. This is not really reading. The speaker who reads for material must concentrate. If he reaches the bottom of a page without an idea, he must go back to get it. It is better not to read too rapidly the first time, in order to save this repetition. The ability to read is trained in exactly the same way as any other ability. Accuracy first, speed later. Perhaps the most prevalent fault of students of all kinds is lack of concentration.

Understanding. After reading comes understanding. To illustrate this, poetry again might be cited, for any one can *read* poetry, though many declare they cannot understand it. The simplest looking prose may be obscure to the mind which is slow in comprehending. When we read we get general ideas, cursory impressions; we catch the drift of the author's meaning. Reading for material must be more thorough than that. It must not merely believe it understands; it must preclude the slightest possibility of misunderstanding.

A reader who finds in a printed speech approval of a system of *representation* but a condemnation of a system of *representatives* must grasp at once, or must work out for himself, the difference between these two: the first meaning a relationship only, the second meaning men serving as delegates. When he meets an unusual word like *mandatory*, he must not be content to guess at its significance by linking it with *command* and *mandate*, for as used in international affairs it means something quite definite. To secure this complete understanding of all his reading he will consult consistently every book of reference. He should read with a good dictionary at his elbow, and an atlas and an encyclopedia within easy reach. If he is able to talk over with others what he reads, explaining to them what is not clear, he will have an excellent method of testing his own understanding. The old-fashioned practice of "saying lessons over" at home contributed to this growth of a pupil's understanding.

Selecting. Third, the reader for material must know how to select. As he usually reads to secure information or arguments for a certain definite purpose, he will save time by knowing quickly what not to read. All that engages his attention without directly contributing to his aim is wasting time and energy. He must learn how to use books. If he cannot handle alphabetized collections quickly he is wasting time. If he does not know how material is arranged he will waste both time and energy. He must know books.

Every printed production worthy of being called a book should have an index. Is the index the same as the table of contents? The table of contents is printed at the beginning of the volume. It is a synopsis, by chapter headings or more detailed topics, of the plan of the book. It gives a general outline of the contents of the book. You are interested in public speaking. You wonder whether a book contains a chapter on debating. Does this one? You notice that a speaker used a series of jerky gesticulations. You wonder whether this book contains a chapter upon gestures. Does it?

The table of contents is valuable for the purposes just indicated. It appears always at the beginning of a work. If the work fills more than one volume, the table of contents is sometimes given for all of them in the first; sometimes it is divided among the volumes; sometimes both arrangements are combined.

The table of contents is never so valuable as the index. This always comes at the end of the book. If the work is in more than one volume the index comes at the *end of the last volume*. What did you learn of the topic *gestures* in this book from your reference to the table of contents? Now look at the index. What does the index do for a topic? If a topic is treated in various parts of a long work the volumes are indicated by Roman numerals, the pages by ordinary numerals.

Interpret this entry taken from the index of *A History of the United States* by H.W. Elson.

> Slavery, introduced into Virginia, i, 93; in South Carolina, 122; in Georgia, 133; in New England, 276; in the South, 276; during colonial period, iii, 69, 70; in Missouri, 72; attacked by the Abolitionists, 142-6; excluded from California, 184; character of, in the South, 208 *seq.*; population, iv, 82; abolished in District of Columbia, in new territories, 208; abolished by Thirteenth Amendment, 320, 321.

Retaining Knowledge. The only valid test of the reader's real equipment is what he retains and can use. How much of what you read do you remember? The answer depends upon education, training in this particular exercise, and lapse of time. What method of remembering do you find most effective in your own case? To answer this you should give some attention to your own mind. What kind of mind have you? Do you retain most accurately what you see? Can you reproduce either exactly or in correct substance what you read to yourself without any supporting aids to stimulate your memory? If you have this kind of mind develop it along that line. Do not weaken its power by letting it lean on any supports at all. If you find you can do without them, do not get into the habit of taking notes. If you can remember to do everything you should do during a trip downtown don't make a list of the items before you go. If you can retain from a single reading the material you are gathering, don't make notes. Impress things upon your memory faculty. Develop that ability in yourself.

Have you a different kind of mind, the kind which remember best what it tells, what it explains, what it does? Do you fix things in your brain by performing them? Does information become rooted in your memory because you have imparted it to others? If so you should secure the material you gather from your reading by adapting some method related to the foregoing. You may talk it over with some one else, you may tell it aloud to yourself, you may imagine you are before an audience and practise impressing them with what you want to retain. Any device which successfully fixes knowledge in your memory is legitimate. You should know enough about your own mental processes to find for yourself the best and quickest way. It is often said of teachers that they do not actually feel that they *know* a subject until they have tried to teach it to others.

Taking Notes. Another kind of mind recalls or remembers material it has read when some note or hint suggests all of it. This kind of mind depends upon the inestimably valuable art of note-taking, a method quite as worthy as the two just considered if its results justify its employment. Note-taking does not mean a helter-skelter series of exclamatory jottings. It means a well-planned, regularly organized series of entries so arranged that reference to any portion recalls vividly and exactly the full material of the original. Books and speeches are well planned. They follow a certain order. Notes based upon them should reproduce that plan and show the relative value of parts.

When completed, such notes, arranged in outline form, should enable the maker to reproduce the extended material from which they were made. If he cannot do that, his reading and his note-taking were to little purpose. A speaker who has carefully written out his full speech and delivers it form the manuscript can use that speech over and over again. But that does not indicate that he really *knows* much about the topic he is discussing. He did know about it once. But the man who from a series of notes can reconstruct material worked up long before proves that he has retained his knowledge of it. Besides, this method gives him the chance to adapt his presentation to the changing conditions and the new audience.

In using this method, when a particularly important bit of information is met, it should be set down very carefully, usually verbatim, as it may be quoted exactly in the speech. This copy may be made upon the paper where the regular notes are being entered so that it may be found later embodied in the material it supports. Or it may later be cut from this sheet to be shifted about and finally fixed when planning the speech, or preparing the outline (discussed in the next two chapters). Many practised speech-makers copy such material upon the regularly sized library catalog cards (3 by 5 inches), some distinguishing by the colors of cards the various kinds of material, such as arguments supporting a position, opposite arguments, refutation, statistics, court judgments, etc. The beginner will find for himself what methods he can use best. Of course he must never let his discriminating system become so elaborate that he consumes unjustifiable time and thought in following its intricate plan.

In all cases of quotations—either verbatim or in resume—the authority must be noted. Author, official title or position, title of work, circumstances, date, volume, page, etc., should be clearly set down. In law cases the date is especially important as so frequently the latest decision reverses all the earlier ones. For convenience of filing and handling these items are placed at the top of the card.

Monroe Doctrine—Meaning

W. Wilson—Hist. Amer. People, V, 245

The U.S. had not undertaken to maintain an actual formal protectorate over the S. Amer. states, but it did frankly undertake to act as their nearest friend in the settlement of controversies with European nations, and

> no President, whether Rep. or Dem., had hesitated since this critical dispute concerning the boundaries of Brit. Guiana arose to urge its settlement upon terms favorable to Venezuela.

The following notes were made by a student in preparation for a speech upon the opposition to the Covenant of the League of Nations. These excerpts are from the notes upon the newspaper reports of the debate in Boston in 1919 between Senator Lodge and President Lowell of Harvard. Notice how accurately they suggest the material of the original. The numbers represent the paragraph numbers.

> Monroe Doctrine.

35. Monroe Doctrine a fence that cannot be extended by taking it down.

36. Monroe Doctrine a corollary of Washington's foreign policy.

37. Geographical considerations on which Monroe Doctrine rested still obtain.

38. Systems of morality and philosophy are not transient, because they rest on verities.

39. Monroe Doctrine rests on law of self-preservation.

40. Offers a larger reservation of Monroe Doctrine as third constructive criticism.

SENATOR LODGE

> What a League should provide.

3. Wants to consider what such a league must contain.

4. Must have provision for obligatory arbitration.

5. Obligation not to resort to war must be compulsory.

6. Compulsion must be such that no nation will venture to incur it.

7. Nation that does not submit to arbitration must be treated as outlaw.

8. If decisions of arbitrations are clear and generally considered just, a nation desiring to wage war should be prevented.

9. Points of contact are not points of friction except when made too infrequent.

10. Travel, intercourse, frequent meetings help amicable adjustments.

11. League should provide councils where men can meet and talk over differences.

12. Penalty for violating agreements should be automatic.

13. All should be obliged to make war on attacking nation.

PRESIDENT LOWELL.

Using the Library. A reader must know how to use libraries. This means he must be able to find books by means of the card catalogs. These are arranged by both authors and subjects. If he knows the author of a book or its title he can easily find the cards and have the book handed to him. Very often he will seek information upon topics entirely new to him. In this case he must look under the entry of the topic for all the books bearing upon his. From the titles, the brief descriptions, and (sometimes) the tables of contents upon the cards he can select intelligently the books he needs. For instance, if he is searching for arguments to support a new kind of city government he could discard at once several books cataloged as follows, while he could pick unerringly the four which might furnish him the material he wants. These books are listed under the general topic "Cities."

The Spirit of Youth and the City Streets. Old English Towns. Municipal Administration. The Modern City and its Problems. Personality of American Cities. Historic Towns of the Southern

States. Romantic Germany. Cities of Italy. American Municipal Progress.

Cross references are also valuable. In addition to books cataloged under the topic consulted, others grouped under other subjects may contain related information. Here are three actual cross references taken from a library catalog.

Land: Ownership, rights, and rent. See also conservation, production, agriculture.

Laboring classes: Morals and habits. See also ethics, amusements, Sunday.

Church. See also church and state, persecutions.

The continual use of a library will familiarize a student with certain classes of books to which he may turn for information. If he is permitted to handle the books themselves upon the shelves he will soon become skilful in using books. Many a trained speaker can run his eye over titles, along tables of contents, scan the pages, and unerringly pick the heart out of a volume. Nearly all libraries now are arranged according to one general plan, so a visitor who knows this scheme can easily find the class of books he wants in almost any library he uses. This arrangement is based upon the following decimal numbering and grouping of subject matter.

LIBRARY CLASSIFICATION

000 to 090, *General works*. Bibliography. Library economy. Cyclopedias. Collections. Periodicals. Societies, museums. Journalism, newspapers. Special libraries, polygraphy. Book rarities.

100 to 190, *Philosophy*. Metaphysics. Special topics. Mind and body. Philosophic systems. Mental faculties, psychology. Logic, dialectics. Ethics. Ancient philosophers. Modern.

200 to 290, *Religion*. Natural Theology. Bible. Doctrinal dogmatics, theology. Devotional, practical. Homiletic, pastoral, parochial. Church, institutions, work. Religious history. Christian churches and sects. Ethnic, non-christian.

300 to 390, *Sociology*. Statistics. Political science. Political economy. Law. Administration. Associations,

institutions. Education. Commerce, communication. Customs, costumes, folklore.

400 to 490, *Philology*. Comparative. English. German. French. Italian. Spanish. Latin. Greek. Minor literatures.

500 to 590, *Natural science*. Mathematics, Astronomy. Physics. Chemistry. Geology. Paleontology. Biology. Botany. Zoölogy.

600 to 690, *Useful arts*. Medicine. Engineering. Agriculture. Domestic economy. Communication, commerce. Chemic technology. Manufactures. Mechanic trades. Building.

700 to 790, *Fine arts*. Landscape gardening. Architecture. Sculpture. Drawing, decoration, design. Painting. Engraving. Photography. Music. Amusements.

800 to 890, *Literature* (same order as under *Philology*, 400).

900 to 990, *History*. Geography and travels. Biography. Ancient history. Modern Europe. Asia. Africa. North America. South America. Oceanica and polar regions.

M. Dewey: *Decimal Classification*

Using Periodicals. In the section on taking notes the direction was given that in citing legal decisions the latest should be secured. Why? That same principle applies to citing any kind of information in a speech. Science, history, politics, government, international questions, change so rapidly in these times that the fact of yesterday is the fiction of today, and *vice versa*. A speaker must be up to date in his knowledge. This he can be only by consulting current periodicals. He cannot read them all so he must use the aids provided for him. The best of these is the *Reader's Guide to Periodical Literature* issued every month and kept in the reference room of all libraries. In it, arranged under both subject and author's name, are listed the articles which have appeared in the various magazines. The December issue contains the entries for the entire year. A group of topics from a recent monthly issue will show its value to the speaker securing material.

> Eastern Question. British case in the East. H. Sidebotham, Asia 19:261-1263 Mr '19.—England and her eastern policy. H. Sidebotham. Asia, 19:158-161. F '19.—Khanates of the Middle East. Ikbal Ali Shah. Contemp. 115:183-187 F '19.—More secret treaties in the Near East. L. Stoddard. Maps. World's Work. 37: 589-591. Mr '19.—Part of the United States in the Near East. R of Rs 59:305-306 Mr '19.—Should America act as trustee of the Near East? Asia, 19:141-144 F'19.

By this time the student speaker will have that mental alertness referred to early in this book. He will be reading regularly some magazine—not to pass the time pleasantly—but to keep himself posted on current topics and questions of general interest, in which the articles will direct him to other periodicals for fuller treatment of the material he is gathering. The nature of some of these is suggested here.

> *The Outlook*, "An illustrated weekly journal of current events."

> *Current Opinion*, Monthly. Review of the World, Persons in the Foreground, Music and Drama, Science and Discovery, Religion and Social Ethics, Literature and Art, The Industrial World, Reconstruction.

> *The Literary Digest*, Weekly. Topics of the Day, Foreign Comment, Science and Invention, Letters and Art, Religion and Social Service, Current Poetry, Miscellaneous, Investments and Finance.

> *The Independent*, an illustrated weekly.

EXERCISES

1. Describe to the class the contents of a recent issue of a magazine. Concentrate upon important departments, articles, or policies, so that you will not deliver a mere list.

2. Tell how an article in some periodical led you to read more widely to secure fuller information.

3. Explain why you read a certain periodical regularly.

4. Speak upon one of the following topics:

> Freak magazines.
> My magazine.
> Policies of magazines.
> Great things magazines have done.
> Technical magazines.
> Adventures at a magazine counter.
> Propaganda periodicals.

5. Explain exactly how you study.

6. How would you secure an interview with some person of prominence?

7. Is the "cramming" process of studying a good one?

8. Is it ever justifiable?

9. Explain how, why, and when it may be used by men in their profession.

10. Give the class an idea of the material of some book you have read recently.

11. Explain how reading a published review or hearing comments on a book induced you to read a volume which proved of value to you.

12. Can you justify the reading of the last part only of a book? Consider non-fiction.

13. For preserving clippings, notes, etc., which method is better—cards filed in boxes or drawers, scrap-books, or slips and clippings grouped in envelopes?

14. Report to the class some information upon one of the following. Tell exactly how and where you secured your information.

Opium traffic in China.
Morphine habit in the United States.
Women in literature.
A drafted army as compared with a volunteer army.
Orpheum as a theater name.
Prominent business women.
War time influence of D'Annunzio.
Increasing cost of living.
Secretarial courses.
The most beautiful city of the American continent.
Alfalfa.
Women surgeons.
The blimp.
Democracy in Great Britain compared with that of the United States.
The root of the Mexican problem.
San Marino.
Illiteracy in the United States.
How women vote.

(NOTE.—The teacher should supply additions, substitutes, and modifications.)

CHAPTER VII

PLANNING THE SPEECH

Selecting Material. It can be assumed, by the time you have reached this point in the study and practice of making speeches, that you have words to express your thoughts and some fair skill of delivery, that you know something about preparing various kinds of introductions and conclusions, that you know how your own mind operates in retaining new information, and that you know how to secure material for various purposes. Either clearly assimilated in your brain or accurately noted upon paper you have all the ideas that are to appear in your speech.

The Length of the Speech. Look over this material again. Consider it carefully in your thoughts, mentally deciding how long a time or how many words you will devote to each topic or entry. Can you from such a practical consideration determine how long in time your speech will be? Are you limited by requirements to a short time as were the Four Minute Speakers? Have you been allotted a half hour? Will you hold your audience longer?

These may appear simple things, but they cover the first essential of planning any speech. It should be just the correct length—neither too long nor too short. Many beginners—timid, hesitant, untrained—will frequently fill too short a time, so that they must drill themselves into planning longer productions. On the other hand, it may be stated, as a general criticism, that many speakers talk too long.

A United States Senator, in order to block the vote on a bill he was opposing, decided to speak until Congress had to adjourn, so he deliberately planned to cover a long time. He spoke for some twenty-two hours. Of course he did not say much, nor did he talk continuously; to get rests, he requested the clerk to call the roll, and while the list was being marked, he ate and drank enough to sustain him. Technically his speech was uninterrupted, for he still had the floor. Though we may not approve of such methods of legislative procedure we must see that for this speech the first element of its plan was its length.

Keep this consideration of time always in mind. Speakers always ask how long they are to speak, or they stipulate how much time they require. Legislative bodies frequently have limiting rules. Courts sometimes allow lawyers so much time. A minister must fit his sermon to the length of the service. A business man must not waste his hearers' time. A lecturer must not tire his audience. In Congress members must be given chances to eat. In Parliament, which meets in the evening, men grow anxious for bed.

Making the Speech too Long. The rule is fundamental, yet it is violated continually. I have known of instances when four men, asked to present material in a meeting announced months in advance as lasting two hours, have totally disregarded this fact, and prepared enough material to consume over an hour each. In such cases the presiding officer should state to each that he will be allowed exactly thirty minutes and no more. He may tap on the table after twenty-five have elapsed to warn the speaker to pass to his conclusion, and at the expiration of the time make him bring his remarks to a close and give way to the next speaker. There is no unfairness in this. The real offense is committed by the speaker who proves himself so inconsiderate, so discourteous of the conditions that he places himself in such an embarrassing circumstance. He deserves only justice tempered by no mercy. I have heard the first of two speakers who were to fill an hour of a commemorative service in a church talk on for an hour and ten minutes, boring the congregation to fidgety restlessness and completely preventing the second speaker—the more important—from delivering a single word.

Mark Twain tells how he went to church one hot night to hear a city mission worker describe his experiences among the poor people of the crowded districts who, though they needed help, were too modest or proud to ask for it. The speaker told of the suffering and bravery he found. Then he pointed out that the best gifts to charity are not the advertised bounties of the wealthy but the small donations of the less fortunate. His appeals worked Mark Twain up to great enthusiasm and generosity. He was ready to give all he had with him—four hundred dollars—and borrow more. The entire congregation wanted to offer all it had. But the missionary kept on talking. The audience began to notice the heat. It became hotter and hotter. They grew more and more uncomfortable. Mark's generosity began to shrink. It dwindled to less and less as the speech lengthened until when the plate did finally reach him, he stole ten cents from it. He adds that this simply proves how a little thing like a long-winded speech can induce crime.

Plan your speech so that it will be the proper length.

Discarding Material. This first consideration very likely indicates to you that you have much more material than you can use in the time allowed or assigned you. You must discard some. Strange as it may seem, this is one of the must difficult directions to carry out. It seems such a waste of time and material to select for actual presentation so small a part of all you have carefully gathered. There is always the temptation to "get it all in somehow." Yet the direction must remain inflexible. You can use only part of it. You must carefully select what will serve your purpose. What is the purpose of your speech? What is the character of your audience? These two things will determine to a large extent, what and how much you must relinquish. Your finished speech will be all the better for the weeding-out process. Better still, in all your preliminary steps for subsequent speeches you will become skilful in selecting while you are gathering the material itself. Finally you will become so practised that you will not burden yourself with waste, although you will always secure enough to supply you with a reserve supply for assurance and emergency.

Relation of Material to the Purpose of the Speech. A few examples will show the wide application of this principle. A boy who has explained to his father the scholarship rules of his school concerning athletes will discard a great deal of that material when he addresses a student gathering. A speaker on child labor in a state where women have voted for a long time will discard much of the material presented in a neighboring state where general franchise has just been granted. If in a series of remarks you want to emphasize the thrilling experience you have had with a large fish which jerked you out of a boat, you would not include such material as the trip on the train to the lake where you had your adventure. Why not?

These are humble instances, but the principle of selection is the same for all speeches.

A man who was asked to lecture on Mark Twain knew the contents of the thirty published volumes written by him, all the biographies, practically every article written about him; he had conversed with people who had known him; he had visited scenes of his life; yet when he planned to talk for an hour he had to reject everything except two striking periods of his life with their effects upon his writing.

Burke, in one great effort, declared he had no intention of dealing with the *right* of taxation; he confined himself merely to the *expediency* of Great Britain's revenue laws for America. Other great speakers have—in their finished speeches—just as clearly indicated the plans they have decided to follow. Such definite announcements determine the material of many introductions.

> My task will be divided under three different heads: first, The Crime Against Kansas, in its origin and extent; secondly, The Apologies for the Crime; and, thirdly, The True Remedy.
>
> CHARLES SUMNER: *The Crime against Kansas*, 1856

> Mr. President and Fellow Citizens of New York:
>
> The facts with which I shall deal this evening are mainly old and familiar; nor is there anything new in the general use I shall make of them. If there shall be any novelty, it will be in the mode of presenting the facts, and the inferences and observations following that presentation. In his speech last autumn at Columbus, Ohio, as reported in the *New York Times*, Senator Douglas said: "Our fathers, when they framed the government under which we live, understood this question just as well, and even better, than we do now."
>
> I fully indorse this, and I adopt it as a text for this discourse. I so adopt it because it furnishes a precise and an agreed starting-point for a discussion between Republicans and that wing of the Democracy headed by Senator Douglas. It simply leaves the inquiry: What was the understanding those fathers had of the question mentioned?
>
> ABRAHAM LINCOLN: *Cooper Union Speech*, 1860

Indicating the Plan in the Speech. In some finished and long speeches parts of the plan are distributed to mark the divisions in the progress of the development. The next quotation shows such an insertion.

> And now sir, against all these theories and opinions, I maintain —
>
> 1. That the Constitution of the United States is not a league, confederacy, or compact between the people of the several States in their sovereign capacities; but a government proper, founded on the adoption of the people, and creating direct relations between itself and individuals.
>
> 2. That no State authority has power to dissolve these relations; that nothing can dissolve them but revolution; and that, consequently, there can be no such thing as secession without revolution.
>
> 3. That there is a supreme law, consisting of the Constitution of the United States, and acts of Congress passed in pursuance of it, and treaties; and that, in cases not capable of assuming the character of a suit in law or equity, Congress must judge of, and finally interpret, this supreme law so often as it has occasion to pass acts of legislation; and in cases capable of assuming, and actually assuming, the character of a suit, the Supreme Court of the United States is the final interpreter.
>
> 4. That an attempt by a State to abrogate, annul, or nullify an act of Congress, or to arrest its operation within her limits, on the ground that, in her opinion, such law is unconstitutional, is a direct usurpation on the just powers of the general Government, and on the equal rights of other States; a plain violation of the Constitution, a proceeding essentially revolutionary in its character and tendency.
>
> Daniel Webster: *The Constitution Not a Compact between Sovereign States*, 1833

Such a statement to the audience is especially helpful when the speaker is dealing with technical subjects, or material with which most people are not usually and widely conversant. Scientific considerations always become clearer when such plans are simply constructed, clearly announced, and plainly followed.

So far as I know, there are only three hypotheses which ever have been entertained, or which well can be entertained, respecting the past history of Nature. I will, in the first place, state the hypotheses, and then I will consider what evidence bearing upon them is in our possession, and by what light of criticism that evidence is to be interpreted. Upon the first hypothesis, the assumption is, that phenomena of Nature similar to those exhibited by the present world have always existed; in other words, that the universe has existed from all eternity in what may be broadly termed its present condition.

The second hypothesis is, that the present state of things has had only a limited duration; and that, at some period in the past, a condition of the world, essentially similar to that which we now know, came into existence, without any precedent condition from which it could have naturally proceeded. The assumption that successive states of Nature have arisen, each without any relation of natural causation to an antecedent state, is a mere modification of this second hypothesis.

The third hypothesis also assumes that the present state of things has had but a limited duration; but it supposes that this state has been evolved by a natural process from an antecedent state, and that from another, and so on; and, on this hypothesis, the attempt to assign any limit to the series of past changes is, usually, given up.

THOMAS H. HUXLEY: *Lectures on Evolution*, 1876

EXERCISES

1. According to what methods are the foregoing plans arranged? Which division in Sumner's speech was the most important? Was he trying to get his listeners to do anything? What do you think that object was?

2. In Lincoln's speech do you think he planned the material chronologically? Historically? What reasons have you for your answer?

3. Which of Webster's four parts is the most important? Give reasons for your answer.

4. Which hypothesis (what does the word mean?) did Huxley himself support? What induces you to think thus? Is this plan in any respect like Sumner's? Explain your answer.

5. Make a list of the ways in which material of speeches may be arranged.

Arrangement. Importance. If you have several topics to cover in a single speech where would you put the most important? First or last? Write upon a piece of paper the position you choose. You have given this plan some thought so you doubtlessly put down the correct position. What did you write? First? That is usually the answer of nine pupils out of every ten. Are you with the majority? If you wrote that the most important topic should be treated first, you are wrong. The speech would be badly planned. Think for a moment. Which should be the most important part of a story or a play? The beginning or the ending? If it is the early part, why should any one read on to the end or stay for the curtain to come down the last time? So in speeches the importance of topics should always increase as the speech proceeds. This, then, is a principle of planning. Arrange your topics in an ascending order of importance. Work up to what is called the climax.

The list you made in response to direction 5 given above should now be presented to the class and its contents discussed. What kind of material is likely to be arranged according to each of your principles? You have put down the chronological order, or the order of time, or some similar phrase. Just what do you mean by that? Do you mean, begin with the earliest material and follow in chronological order down to the latest? Could the reverse order ever be used? Can you cite some instance? Is contrast a good order to follow in planning? Cite material which could be so arranged. Would an arrangement from cause to effect be somewhat like one based on time? Explain your answer. Under what circumstances do you think the opposite might be used—from effect to cause?

While there are almost countless methods of arrangements—for any one used in one part of a speech may be combined with any other in some different portion—the plan should always be determined by three fundamental matters; the material itself, the audience to which it is to be presented, and the effect the speaker wants to produce.

Even during this preliminary planning of the speech the author must be careful that when his arrangement is decided upon it possesses the three qualities necessary to every good composition. These three are unity, coherence, and emphasis.

Unity. Unity explains itself. A speech must be about one single thing. A good speech produces one result. It induces action upon one single point. It allows no turning aside from its main theme. It does not stray from the straight and narrow road to pick flowers in the adjacent fields, no matter how enticing the temptation to loiter may be. In plain terms it does not admit as part of its material anything not closely and plainly connected with it. It does not step aside for everything that crops into the speaker's mind. It advances steadily, even when not rapidly. It does not "back water." It goes somewhere.

To preserve unity of impression a speaker must ruthlessly discard all material except that which is closely associated with his central intention. He must use only that which contributes to his purpose. The same temptation to keep unrelated material—if it be good in itself—will be felt now as when the other unsuitable material was set aside.

This does not prevent variety and relief. Illustrative and interesting minor sections may be, at times must be, introduced. But even by their vividness and attractiveness they must help the speech, not hinder it. The decorations and ornaments must never be allowed to detract from the utility of the composition.

Unity may be damaged by admitting parts not in the direct line of the theme. It may be violated by letting minor portions become too long. The illustration may grow so large by the introduction of needless details that it makes the listeners forget the point it was designed to enforce. Or it may be so far-fetched as to bear no real relation to the thread of development. Here lies the pitfall of the overworked "funny," story, introduced by "that reminds me." Too often it is not humorous enough to justify repetition; or—what is worse—it does not fit into the circumstances. Another fault of many speakers is over-elaboration of expression, not only for non-essentials, but in the important passages as well. Involved language demands explanation. The attempts to clear up what should have been simply said at first may lead a speaker to devote too many words to a single point.

This matter of unity must not be misunderstood as prohibiting the inclusion of more than one topic in a speech. A legislator in urging the repeal of a law might have several topics, such as how the law was passed, its first operations, its increasing burdens upon people, the disappearance of the necessity for it, better methods of securing the same or better results, etc., yet all grouped about the motivating theme of securing the repeal of the law. To emphasize the greatness of a man's career a speaker might introduce such topics as his obscure origin, his unmarked youth, the spur that stimulated his ambition, his early reverses, provided that they contribute to the impression intended, to make vivid his real achievements.

In early attempts at delivering speeches don't be afraid to pause at certain places to consider whether what you are about to say really contributes to the unity or destroys it. Aside from helping you to think upon your feet, this mental exercise will help your speech by making you pause at times—a feature of speaking often entirely disregarded by many persons.

Coherence. The second quality a finished composition should have is coherence. If you know what *cohere* and *cohesion* mean (perhaps you have met these words in science study) you have the germ of the term's meaning. It means "stick-together-itive-ness." The parts of a speech should be so interrelated that every part leads up to all that follows. Likewise every part develops naturally from all that goes before, as well as what immediately precedes. There must be a continuity running straight through the material from start to finish. Parts should be placed where they fit best. Each portion should be so placed—at least, in thought—that all before leads naturally and consistently up to it, and it carries on the thread to whatever follows. This prevents rude breaks in the development of thought. Skilfully done, it aids the hearer to remember, because so easily did the thought in the speech move from one point to another, that he can carry the line of its progression with him long after. So the attainment of coherence in a speech contributes directly to that desired end—a deep impression.

Incoherent speeches are so mainly because of absence of plan, whether they be short or long, conversational or formal.

Emphasis. The third quality a speech should have is emphasis. Applied to a connected sequence of words this means that what is of most importance shall stand out most forcefully; that what is not so important shall show its subordinate relation by its position, its connection with what goes before and after; that what is least important shall receive no emphasis beyond its just due. Such manipulation requires planning and rearranging, careful weighing of the relative importance of all portions. Recall what was said of the place of the most important part.

Throughout the speech there must also be variety of emphasis. It would not be fitting to have everything with a forceful emphasis upon it. To secure variation in emphasis you must remember that in speeches the best effects will be made upon audiences by offering them slight relief from too close attention or too impressive effects. If you observe the plans finally followed by good speakers you will be able to see that they have obeyed this suggestion. They have the power to do what is described as "swaying the audience." In its simplest form this depends upon varying the emphasis.

In making an appeal for funds for destitute portions of Europe a telling topic would surely be the sufferings of the needy. Would it be wise to dwell upon such horrors only? Would a humorous anecdote of the happy gratitude of a child for a cast-off toy be good to produce emphasis? Which would make the most emphatic ending—the absolute destitution, the amount to be supplied, the relief afforded, or the happiness to donors for sharing in such a worthy charity? You can see how a mere mental planning, or a shuffling of notes, or a temporary numbering of topics will help in clearing up this problem of how to secure proper and effective emphasis.

Making the First Plan. It would be a helpful thing at this point in the planning to make a pencil list of the topics to be included. This is not a final outline but a mere series of jottings to be changed, discarded, and replaced as the author considers his material and his speech. It is hardly more than an informal list, a scrap of paper. In working with it, don't be too careful of appearances. Erase, cross out, interline, write in margins, draw lines and arrows to carry portions from one place to another, crowd in at one place, remove from another, cut the paper sheets, paste in new parts, or pin slips together. Manipulate your material. Mold it to suit your purposes. Make it follow your plan. By this you will secure a good plan. If this seems a great deal to do, compare it with the time and energy required to learn how to swim, how to play a musical instrument, how to "shoot" in basketball, how to act a part in a play.

Knowing how to speak well is worth the effort. Every time you plan a speech these steps will merge into a continuous process while you are gathering the material. In informal discussion upon topics you are familiar with, you will become able to arrange a plan while you are rising to your feet.

Transitions. As this preliminary plan takes its form under your careful consideration of the material you will decide that there are places between topics or sections which will require bridging over in order to attain coherence and emphasis. These places of division should be filled by transitions. A transition is a passage which carries over the meaning from what precedes to what follows. It serves as a connecting link. It prevents the material from falling apart. It preserves the continuity of ideas. A transition may be as short as a single word, such as *however, consequently, nevertheless*. It may be a sentence. It may grow into a paragraph.

The purpose of transitions—to link parts together—may induce beginners to consider them as of little importance since they manifestly add no new ideas to the theme. This opinion is entirely erroneous. Even in material for reading, transitions are necessary. In material to be received through the ear they are the most valuable helps that can be supplied to have the listener follow the development. They mark the divisions for him. They show that a certain section is completed and a new one is about to begin. They show the relation in meaning of two portions.

The shorter forms of transitions—words and phrases—belong rather to the expression, the language, of the speech than to this preliminary planning.

A speaker should never fail to use such phrases as *on the other hand, continuing the same line of reasoning, passing to the next point, from a different point of view*, because they so clearly indicate the relation of two succeeding passages of a speech.

In planning, the speaker frequently has to consider the insertion of longer transitions—paragraphs or even more extended passages. Just how such links appear in finished speeches the following extracts show. In the first selection Washington when he planned his material realized he had reached a place where he could conclude. He wanted to add more. What reason should he offer his audience for violating the principle discussed in the chapter on conclusions? How could he make clear to them his desire to continue? We cannot assert that he actually did this, but he might have jotted down upon the paper bearing a first scheme of his remarks the phrase, "my solicitude for the people." That, then, was the germ of his transition paragraph. Notice how clearly the meaning is expressed. Could any hearer fail to comprehend? The transition also announces plainly the topic of the rest of the speech.

> Here, perhaps, I ought to stop. But a solicitude for your welfare, which cannot end but with my life, and the apprehension of danger, natural to that solicitude, urge me on an occasion like the present, to offer to your solemn contemplation, and to recommend to your frequent review, some sentiments which are the result of much reflection, of no inconsiderable observation, and which appear to me all-important to the permanency of your felicity as a people. These will be offered to you with the more freedom, as you can only see in them the disinterested warnings of a parting friend, who can possibly have no personal motive to bias his counsels. Nor can I forget, as an encouragement to it, your indulgent reception of my sentiment on a former and not dissimilar occasion.
>
> GEORGE WASHINGTON: *Farewell Address*, 1796

The next selection answers to a part of the plan announced in a passage already quoted in this chapter. Notice how this transition looks both backward and forward: it is both retrospective and anticipatory. If you recall that repetition helps to emphasize facts, you will readily understand why a transition is especially valuable if it adheres to the same language as the first statement of the plan. In a written scheme this might have appeared under the entry, "pass from 1 to 2; list 4 apologies for crime." This suggests fully the material of the passage.

> And with this exposure I take my leave of the Crime against Kansas. Emerging from all the blackness of this Crime, where we seem to have been lost, as in a savage wood, and turning our backs upon it, as upon desolation and death, from which, while others have suffered, we have escaped, I come now to the Apologies which the Crime has found....
>
> They are four in number, and fourfold in character. The first is the Apology tyrannical; the second, the Apology imbecile; the third, the Apology absurd; and the fourth, the Apology infamous. That is all. Tyranny, imbecility, absurdity, and infamy all unite to dance, like the weird sisters, about this Crime.
>
> The Apology tyrannical is founded on the mistaken act of Governor Reeder, in authenticating the Usurping Legislature, etc.
>
> CHARLES SUMNER: The Crime against Kansas, 1856

The beginning speaker should not hesitate to make his transitions perfectly clear to his audience. When they add to the merely bridging use the additional value of serving as short summaries of what has gone before and as sign posts of what is to follow, they are trebly serviceable. The attempt to be clear will seldom be waste of time or effort. The obvious statements of the preceding selections, the use of figures, are excellent models for speakers to imitate. With practice will come skill in making transitions of different kinds, in which the same purposes will be served in various other ways, in what may be considered more finished style. The next extracts represent this kind of transition.

> Sir, like most questions of civil prudence, this is neither black nor white, but gray. The system of copyright has great advantages and great disadvantages; and it is our business to ascertain what these are, and then to make an arrangement under which the advantages may be as far as possible secured, and the

disadvantages as far as possible excluded. The charge which I bring against my honorable and learned friend's bill is this, that it leaves the advantages nearly what they are at present, and increases the disadvantages at least fourfold.

THOMAS B. MACAULAY: *Copyright Bill*, 1841

One-third of the population of the South is of the Negro race. No enterprise seeking the material, civil, or moral welfare of this section can disregard this element of our population and reach the highest success. I but convey to you, Mr. President and Directors, the sentiment of the masses of my race when I say that in no way have the value and manhood of the American Negro been more fittingly and generously recognized than by the managers of this magnificent Exposition at every stage of its progress. It is a recognition that will do more to cement the friendship of the two races than any occurrence since the dawn of our freedom.

BOOKER T. WASHINGTON in a speech at the Atlanta Exposition, 1895

Thinking before You Speak. While students may feel that the steps outlined here demand a great deal of preparation before the final speech is delivered, the explanation may be given that after all, this careful preparation merely carries out the homely adage—think before you speak. If there were more thinking there would be at once better speaking. Anybody can talk. The purpose of studying is to make one a better speaker. The anticipation of some relief may be entertained, for it is comforting to know that after one has followed the processes here explained, they move more rapidly, so that after a time they may become almost simultaneous up to the completion of the one just discussed—planning the speech. It is also worth knowing that none of this preliminary work is actually lost. Nor is it unseen. It appears in the speech itself. The reward for all its apparent slowness and exacting deliberation is in the clearness, the significance of the speech, its reception by the audience, its effect upon them, and the knowledge by the speaker himself that his efforts are producing results in his accomplishments.

All speakers plan carefully for speeches long in advance.

A famous alumnus of Yale was invited to attend a banquet of Harvard graduates. Warned that he must "speak for his dinner" he prepared more than a dozen possible beginnings not knowing of course, in what manner the toastmaster would call upon him. The remainder of his speech was as carefully planned, although not with so many possible choices. Note that from each possible opening to the body of the speech he had to evolve a graceful transition.

Edmund Burke, in his great speech on conciliation with the American colonies, related that some time before, a friend had urged him to speak upon this matter, but he had hesitated. True, he had gone so far as to throw "my thoughts into a sort of parliamentary form"—that is, he made a plan or an outline, but the passage of a certain bill by the House of Commons seemed to have taken away forever the chance of his using the material. The bill, however, was returned from the House of Lords with an amendment and in the resulting debate he delivered the speech he had already planned.

Daniel Webster said that his reply to Hayne had been lying in his desk for months already planned, merely waiting the opportunity or need for its delivery.

Henry Ward Beecher, whose need for preliminary preparation was reduced to its lowest terms, and who himself was almost an instantaneous extemporizer, recognized the need for careful planning by young speakers and warned them against "the temptation to slovenliness in workmanship, to careless and inaccurate statement, to repetition, to violation of good taste."

Slovenliness in planning is as bad as slovenliness in expression.

EXERCISES

Choose any topic suggested in this book. Make a short preliminary plan of a speech upon it. Present it to the class. Consider it from the following requirements:

    1. Does it show clearly its intention?

2. How long will the speech be?

3. Too long? Too short?

4. For what kind of audience is it intended?

5. Has it unity?

6. Has it coherence?

7. Where are transitions most clearly needed?

8. What suggestions would you make for rearranging any parts?

9. What reasons have you for these changes?

10. Is proper emphasis secured?

CHAPTER VIII

MAKING THE OUTLINE OR BRIEF

Orderly Arrangement. A speech should have an orderly arrangement. The effect upon an audience will be more easily made, more deeply impressed, more clearly retained, if the successive steps of the development are so well marked, so plainly related, that they may be carried away in a hearer's understanding. It might be said that one test of a good speech is the vividness with which its framework is discernible. Hearers can repeat outlines of certain speeches. Those are the best. Of others they can give merely confused reports. These are the badly constructed ones.

The way to secure in the delivered speech this delight of orderly arrangement is by making an outline or brief. Most pupils hate to make outlines. The reason for this repugnance is easily understood. A teacher directs a pupil to make an outline before he writes a composition or delivers a speech. The pupil spends hours on the list of entries, then submits his finished theme or address. He feels that the outline is disregarded entirely. Sometimes he is not even required to hand it to the instructor. He considers the time he has spent upon the outline as wasted. It is almost impossible to make him feel that his finished product is all the better because of this effort spent upon the preliminary skeleton, so that in reality his outline is not disregarded at all, but is judged and marked as embodied in the finished article. Most students carry this mistaken feeling about outlines to such an extent that when required to hand in both an outline and a finished composition they will write in haphazard fashion the composition first, and then from it try to prepare the outline, instead of doing as they are told, and making the outline first. It is easier—though not as educating or productive of good results—to string words together than it is to do what outline-making demands—to think.

Professional Writers' Use of Outlines. Professional writers realize the helpfulness of outline-making and the time it saves. Many a magazine article has been sold before a word of the finished manuscript was written.

1

The contributor submitted an outline from which the editor contracted for the finished production. Many a play has been placed in the same form. Books are built up in the same manner. The ubiquitous moving-picture scenario is seldom produced in any other manner.

Macaulay advised a young friend who asked how to keep his brain active to read a couple of solid books, making careful outlines of their material at the same time. One of these should be—if possible—a work in a foreign tongue, so that the strangeness of the language would necessitate slow, careful reading and close thinking. All good students know that the best way to prepare for an examination is to make outlines of all the required reading and study.

It is just because the making of the outline demands such careful thinking that it is one of the most important steps in the production of a speech.

The Outline in the Finished Speech. If the outline really shows in the finished speech, let us see if we can pick the entries out from a portion of one. Edmund Burke in 1775 tried to prevent Great Britain from using coercive measures against the restive American colonies. Many Englishmen were already clamoring for war when Burke spoke in Parliament upon conciliating the Colonies.

I am sensible, Sir, that all which I have asserted in my detail, is admitted in the gross; but that quite a different conclusion is drawn from it. America, gentlemen say, is a noble object. It is an object well worth fighting for. Certainly it is, if fighting a people be the best way of gaining them. Gentlemen in this respect will be led to their choice of means by their complexions and their habits. Those who understand the military art, will of course have some predilection for it. Those who wield the thunder of the state, may have more confidence in the efficacy of arms. But I confess, possibly for want of this knowledge, my opinion is much more in favor of prudent management, than of force; considering force not as an odious, but a feeble instrument, for preserving a people so numerous, so active, so growing, so spirited as this, in a profitable and subordinate connexion with us.

First, Sir, permit me to observe, that the use of force alone is but *temporary*. It may subdue for a moment; but it does not remove the necessity of subduing again; and a nation is not governed which is perpetually to be conquered.

My next objection is its *uncertainty*. Terror is not always the effect of force; and an armament is not a victory. If you do not succeed, you are without resource; for, conciliation failing, force remains; but, force failing, no further hope of reconciliation is left. Power and authority are sometimes bought by kindness; but they can never be begged as alms by an impoverished and defeated violence.

A further objection to force is, that you *impair the object* by your very endeavors to preserve it. The thing you fought for is not the thing which you recover; but depreciated, sunk, wasted, and consumed in the contest. Nothing less will content me, than *whole America*. I do not choose to consume its strength along with our own; because in all parts it is the British strength that I consume. I do not choose to be caught by a foreign enemy at the end of this exhausting conflict, and still less in the midst of it. I may escape; but I can make no assurance against such an event. Let me add, that I do not choose wholly to break the American spirit; because it is the spirit that has made the country.

Lastly, we have no sort of *experience* in favor of force as an instrument in the rule of our colonies. Their growth and their utility has been owing to methods altogether different. Our ancient indulgence has been said to be pursued to a fault. It may be so. But we know if feeling is evidence that our fault was more tolerable than our attempt to mend it; and our sin far more salutary than our penitence.

These, Sir, are my reasons for not entertaining that high opinion of untried force, by which many gentlemen, for whose sentiments in other particulars I have great respect, seem to be so greatly captivated. But there is still behind a third consideration concerning this object, which serves to determine my opinion on the sort of policy which ought to be pursued in the management of America, even more than its population and its commerce, I mean its *temper and character*.

EDMUND BURKE: *Conciliation with America*, 1775

Reconstructing the Outline. In the preliminary arrangement Burke knew that he was going to give his reasons against the use of military force. In his first plan he may not have decided just where he was going to place his four arguments. So they very likely appeared as four topic entries:

Against use of force.
   1. temporary
   2. uncertain
   3. damages America
   4. no experience

Notice that these are jottings to suggest the germs of the arguments. When Burke revised this section he may have changed the expression to indicate more certainty.

Force should not be used against the colonies, because:
   1. it is only temporary

2. it is uncertain in its results
3. it would damage the wealth of the colonies
4. it is based on no experience of Great Britain with
   colonies

Of course, a practised statesman would not have to analyze farther, perhaps not so far, but to illustrate for a student how he might build up his outline, let us analyze one degree farther. Just what is meant by such terms as *temporary, uncertain?* Under each statement, then, might be added a detailed explanation. The finished part of the outline would then appear somewhat like this.

Force should not be used against the colonies, because:
    1. it is only temporary, for
        a. though it subdue for a time, it would have to
            be used again.
    2. it is uncertain in its results, for
        a. Great Britain might not subdue the colonies.
    3. it would damage the wealth of the colonies, for
        a. we would fight to retain a wealthy land, yet
            after the war we should have a ruined one.
    4. it is based on no experience of Great Britain with
      colonies, for
          a. Great Britain has always been indulgent
             rather than severely strict.

Speaking or writing from such a detailed outline as this, consider how much thinking has already been done. With these entries under his eye the speaker need think only of the phrasing of his remarks. He would feel perfectly certain that he would not wander from his theme. Notice how the ideas can be emphasized. The suggestion of damage can be expressed in *impair the object*, and in *depreciated, sunk, wasted, consumed.*

So far this outline—though it covers all its own material—does not indicate the place at which it shall be used in the speech. It could be used near the conclusion where Burke planned to answer all the supporters of plans other than his own. That would be a good place for it. But Burke found a better one. He separated this from his other remarks against his opponents, and brought it in much earlier, thereby linking it with what it most concerned, emphasizing it, and disposing of it entirely so far as his speech was concerned. He had just enumerated the wealth of the colonies as represented by their commerce. He knew that the war party would argue, "If America is so wealthy, it is worth fighting for." That was the place, then, to refute them. To introduce his material he had to make clear the transition from the colonial wealth to his arguments. Notice how plainly the first paragraph quoted here does this. Having given his four reasons against the use of force, notice that he must bring his audience back to the theme he has been discussing. The last paragraph does this in a masterly manner. He has cited two facts about the colonies. To make understanding doubly certain he repeats them—population and commerce—and passes to the next, plainly numbering it as the third.

This recital of the process is not an account of what actually took place in Burke's preparation, but it will give to the student the method by which great speakers *may* have proceeded; we do know that many did follow such a scheme. No amateur who wants to make his speeches worth listening to should omit this helpful step of outline or brief making. Whether he first writes out his speeches in full, or composes them upon his feet, every speaker should prepare an outline or brief of his material. This is a series of entries, so condensed and arranged as to show the relative significance of all the parts of the speech in the proper order of development.

Outline, Brief, Legal Brief. An outline contains entries which are merely topics, not completed statements or sentences.

A brief contains completed statements (sentences).

A legal brief is a formally prepared document (often printed) submitted to a certain court before a case is tried, showing the material the lawyer intends to produce, citing all his authorities, suggesting interpretations of laws and legal decisions to support his contentions, and giving all his conclusions. It is prepared for the use of the court, to reduce the labor in examining records, etc. Practice in the drawing up of such briefs is an important phase of legal study.

The Outline. An outline may recall to a person's mind what he already has learned, but it is seldom definite and informative enough to be as helpful as a brief. A good distinction of the two—besides the one respecting the forms already given—is that the outline represents the point of view of the speaker while the brief represents that of the hearer. Consider again the analyses of Burke in this chapter. Notice that the first list does not give nearly so clear an idea of what Burke actually said as the third. A person seeing only the first might *guess* at what the speaker intended to declare. A person who looked at the third could not fail to *know exactly* the opinions of the speaker and the arguments supporting them.

Pupils frequently make this kind of entry:

Introduction—Time
              Place
              Characters

The main objections to such an outline are that it tells nothing definite, and that it might fit a thousand compositions. Even an outline should say more than such a list does.

In one edition of Burke's speech the page from which the following is quoted is headed "Brief." Is it a brief?

Part II. How to deal with America.

    A. Introduction.
    B. First alternative and objections.
    C. Second alternative and objections.
    D. Third alternative.
    E. Introduction.
    F. Considerations.

        1. Question one of policy, not of abstract right.
        2. Trade laws.
        3. Constitutional precedents.
        4. Application of these.

The Brief. One of the shortest briefs on record was prepared by Abraham Lincoln for use in a suit to recover $200 for the widow of a Revolutionary veteran from an agent who had retained it out of $400 pension money belonging to her. It formed the basis of his speech in court.

> No contract.—Not professional services.—Unreasonable charge.—Money retained by Def't not given to Pl'ff.—Revolutionary War.—Describe Valley Forge privations.—Pl'ff's husband.—Soldier leaving for army.—*Skin Def't.*—Close.

The following will give some idea of the form and definiteness of briefs for debate.

CAPITAL PUNISHMENT

Resolved: That capital punishment should be abolished.[3]

Brief for the Affirmative

I. Capital punishment is inexpedient.
   (*a*) It is contrary to the tendency of civilization.
   (*b*) It fails to protect society.
      (1) It does not prevent murder.
      (2) New crimes follow hard on executions.
   (*c*) It makes punishment uncertain.
      (1) Many criminals are acquitted who would
        be convicted if the penalty were imprisonment.
   (*d*) It is not reformatory.

II. Capital punishment is immoral.
   (*a*) It rests on the old idea of retribution.
   (*b*) It tends to weaken the sacredness of human life.
   (*c*) It endangers the lives of innocent people.
   (*d*) Executions and the sensational newspaper
      accounts which follow have a corrupting influence.

III. Capital punishment is unjust.
   (*a*) Its mistakes are irremediable.
   (*b*) Many men are criminals from force of
      circumstances.
      (1) From heredity.

      (2) From environment.
    (*c*) Inequalities in administration are marked.
        (1) In some states men are hung, in others
           imprisoned for the same crime.

[3] Taken from Brookings and Ringwalt: *Briefs for Debate*, Longmans, Green and Co., where specific references of material for many of the topics are given, as well as general references for the entire subject.

        (2) Many jurors have conscientious scruples
           against condemning a man to death.
        (3) Men of wealth and influence are rarely
           convicted.

IV. The abolition of capital punishment has been followed
    by satisfactory results,
  (*a*) In Europe.
      (1) Russia.
      (2) Switzerland.
      (3) Portugal.
      (4) Belgium.
      (5) Holland.
      (6) Finland.
  (*b*) In the United States.
      (1) Michigan.
      (2) Rhode Island.
      (3) Maine.
      (4) Wisconsin.

Brief for the Negative

I. Capital punishment is permissible.
  (*a*) It has the sanction of the Bible.
      (1) Genesis ix, 2-6.
  (*b*) It has the sanction of history.
      (1) It has been in vogue since the beginning
         of the world.

(*c*) It has the sanction of reason.

    (1) The most fitting punishment is one equal and similar to the injury inflicted.

II. Capital punishment is expedient.

  (*a*) It is necessary to protect society from anarchy and private revenge.

    (1) Death is the strongest preventative of crime.

  (*b*) No sufficient substitute has been offered.

    (1) Life imprisonment is a failure.

    (2) Few serve the sentence.

  (*c*) Its abolition has not been successful.

    (1) In Rhode Island.

    (2) In Michigan.

III. The objections made to capital punishment are not sound.

  (*a*) Prisons are not reformatory.

  (*b*) The fact that crimes have decreased in some places where executions have stopped is not a valid argument.

    (1) All causes which increase the moral well-being of the race decrease crime.

  (*c*) The objection that the innocent suffer is not strong.

    (1) The number of innocent thus suffering is inconsiderable when compared with the great number of murders prevented.

  (*d*) The objection that the penalty is uncertain may be overcome by making it certain.

A few paragraphs back it was said that an outline or brief shows the relative significance of all the parts of a speech. This is done by a systematic use of margins and symbols. From the quoted forms in this chapter certain rules can easily be deduced.

Margins. The speech will naturally divide into a few main parts. These can be designated by spaces and general titles such as introduction, body, development, main argument, answer to opposing views, conclusion. Other captions will be suggested by various kinds of material. Main topics next in importance are placed the farthest to the left, making the first margin. A reader can run his eye down this line and pick out all the main topics of equal importance. Entries just subordinate to these are put each on a separate line, starting slightly to the right. This separation according to connection and value is continued as long as the maker has any minor parts to represent in the brief. It should not be carried too far, however, for the purpose of the entries is to mark clearness and accuracy. If the helping system becomes too elaborate and complicated it destroys its own usefulness.

It is perfectly plain that such an outline might be made and be quite clear, without the addition of any symbols at all, especially if it was short.

Discrimination in the use of words is secured by

The study of synonyms
               antonyms
               homonyms
and care in employing them.

Symbols. Some scheme of marking the entries is a great help. There is no fixed system. Every student may choose from among the many used. If there are many main topics it might be a mistake to use Roman numerals (I, XVIII) as few people can read them quickly enough to follow their sequence. Capital letters may serve better to mark the sequences, but they do not indicate the numerical position. For instance, most of us do not know our alphabets well enough to translate a main topic marked N into the fourteenth point. By combinations of Roman numerals, capitals, usual (Arabic) numerals, small letters, parentheses, enough variety to serve any student purpose can easily be arranged.

The following are samples of systems used.

Specimen 1

Introduction
Argument

I————————————————————————————————
  A——————————————————————————————
    1————————————————————————————
      a————————————————————————
      b————————————————————————
      c————————————————————————
        (1)————————————————————
        (2)————————————————————
        (3)————————————————————
    2————————————————————————————
  B——————————————————————————————
    1————————————————————————————
    2————————————————————————————
II————————————————————————————————-

Conclusion

Specimen 2

A————————————————————————————————
  I——————————————————————————————
    a————————————————————————————
      1————————————————————————
      2————————————————————————
    b————————————————————————————
  II—————————————————————————————-
    a————————————————————————————
    b————————————————————————————
    c————————————————————————————
      1————————————————————————
      2————————————————————————
      3————————————————————————

Specimen 3

1——————————————————————

  1^1————————————————————

  2^1————————————————————

    a^1——————————————————

    b^1——————————————————

    c^1——————————————————

2——————————————————————

  1^2————————————————————

  2^2————————————————————

    a^2——————————————————

    b^2——————————————————

    c^2——————————————————

3——————————————————————

  1^3————————————————————

  2^3————————————————————

Tabulations. With unusual kinds of material and for special purposes there may be value in evolving other forms of outlines. A technically trained person accustomed to reading tabulated reports with hosts of figures to interpret might find a statistical statement at times better suited to his needs. Such tabulations are not any easier to prepare than the regular brief. In fact to most people they are infinitely more difficult to get into form and almost beyond speedy comprehension afterwards. The following is a good illustration of a simple one well adapted to the speaker's purpose—a report of the objections to the first published covenant of the League of Nations. He knew the material of his introduction and conclusion so well that he did not represent them in his carefully arranged sheet. The form was submitted as regular work in a public speaking class and was spoken from during more than forty minutes.

CRITICISMS OF PROPOSED COVENANT OF LEAGUE OF NATIONS

1.--Draft indefinite and loosely written.	Lg Lo Sp Tt Br Hu
2.--Should have clause-	Lo

limiting powers to those specifically granted.						
3.--Proportion of votes required for action of Council not generally stated--should be unanimous.	Lg		Sp	Tt		Hu
4.--Should have clause reserving the Monroe Doctrine.	Lg	Lo	Sp	Tt	Br	Hu
5.--Should state that no nation can be required to become a mandatory without its consent.	Lg	Lo			Br	Hu
6.--Should have provision for withdrawals.	Lg	Lo	Sp	Tt		Hu
7.--Jurisdiction of League over internal affairs (immigration, tariffs, coastwise trade) should be expressly excluded.	Lg				Br	Hu
8.--Terms of admission of other nations too strict.					Br	
9.--Basis of representation not fair.					Br	
10.--Provision should be made for expansion of nations by peaceable means.					Br	
11.--Each nation should have right to decide whether it will follow advice of Council as to use of force.					Br	
12.--Each nation should have right to determine whether it will boycott delinquent nations.					Br	

> Note:--items 11 and 12 are apparently directed against Art. XVI containing the Ipso Facto clause and Art. X.
>
> 13.--Should not guarantee the integrity and independence of Lg all members of the league.   Hu

Above criticisms taken from published statements of

  Messrs. Lodge
        Lowell
        Spencer
        Taft
        Bryan
        Hughes
(denoted respectively Lg, Lo, Sp, Tt, Br and Hu).

Authorities in the Brief. Authorities for the statements made in the brief may be put into parentheses, if they are to be included. Such further devices will suggest themselves to students. In addition to such markings as here listed, some men who use many outlines emphasize upon them details which they may have to find quickly by underlining the symbol or first word with colored pencil. Such a device is especially valuable to a technical expert whose system could be uniform through the outlines of all his reports, etc. Or a lecturer with so much time to fill may mark upon the outline 1/4, 1/2, 3/4, to indicate to himself that his material is being covered at a proper rate to correspond with the time. He might put in *15 min.* or *30 min.* or *45 min.* if he was to speak for an hour. The first division is the better, for he might be required to condense a twenty-minute speech to ten.

Selections for Briefing. Before the student makes many briefs of his own he should work in the other direction by outlining material already in existence so that he can be assured he knows main topics from minor ones, important issues from subordinate reasons, headings from examples. If all the members of the class outline the same material the resulting discussion will provide additional exercise in speaking in explanation or support of an

1

interpretation. After the teacher and class together have made one, the students should work independently.

EXERCISES

Besides the extracts quoted here others should be supplied. Editorials from a single issue of a newspaper can easily be secured by the entire class for this work. A chapter from a book may be assigned.

1. INCIDENTS OF GOVERNMENT TRADING

An expert before the President's street railway commission of inquiry testified that he disapproved of public ownership and operation theoretically, but approved it practically, because it was the quickest and surest way of making people sick of it. Otherwise he thought that education of the public out of its favor for high costs and low profits by public utilities would require a generation, and the present emergency calls for prompt relief.

New York City has just resolved to build with its own funds a Coney Island bathhouse, and has on file an offer to build it with private money at a cost of $300,000, with a guarantee of 15-cent baths. Accepting no responsibility for the merits of the private bidder's proposal, it does not appear likely that the city can supply cheaper baths or give more satisfaction to bathers than a management whose profits were related to its efforts to please patrons. On the other hand, it is sure that the city's financial embarrassment is due to supplying many privileges at the cost of the taxpayers, which might have been supplied both more cheaply and better by private enterprise with profit than by the city without profit, and with the use of ill-spared public funds.

New York does not stand alone in these misadventures, which are warnings against trading by either local or national government. Take, for example, the manner in which the army is disposing of its surplus blankets, as reported from Boston. A Chicago firm which wished to bid was permitted to inspect three samples of varying grades, but a guarantee that the goods sold would correspond to the samples was refused. The bales could neither be opened nor allowed to be opened, nor would information be given whether the blankets in the bales were cotton, wool, or mixed, whether single or double, whether bed blankets or regulation army blankets. The likelihood that the Government will get the worth of its blankets is small. There may be unknown reasons for such uncommercial procedure, but what shall be said of the fact that at the same time that these blankets are being sold the Interior Department is asking for bids to supply 10,000 blankets for the Indians? The reason for buying more when there is an embarrassing over-supply is that the specifications call for the words "Interior Department" to be woven into the blankets. To an outsider it would seem that the words might be indelibly stamped on the old blankets of similar description, and that the departure from custom would be better than the loss on the old blankets and the increased expenditure for the new blankets.

The reason for mentioning such incidents is that there are so many more of which the public never hears. Their combined educative effect would be great, but it is wasted without publicity. Since the public is not unanimous against public ownership and operation, there must be a considerable number of persons who are proof against anything but a catastrophe greater than the prostration of the railway and utility industries. That is an expansive way of education, but perhaps Dr. Cooley, Dean of the University of Michigan, is right in his view that the method is necessary to prevent a greater calamity by persistence in the error.

New York Times, July 21, 1919

2. Fourscore and seven years ago our Fathers brought forth on this continent a new nation, conceived in liberty, and dedicated to the proposition that all men are created equal.

Now we are engaged in a great civil war, testing whether that nation or any nation so conceived or so dedicated, can long endure. We are met on a great battlefield of that war. We have come to dedicate a portion of that field as a final resting place for those who here gave their lives that that nation might live. It is altogether fitting and proper that we should do this.

But, in a larger sense, we cannot dedicate—we cannot consecrate—we cannot hallow this ground. The brave men, living and dead, who struggled here, have consecrated it far above our poor power to add or detract. The world will little note nor long remember what we say here, but it can never forget what they did here. It is for us, the living, rather, to be here dedicated to the unfinished work which they who fought here have thus far so nobly advanced. It is rather for us to be here dedicated to the great task remaining before us—that from these honored dead we take increased devotion to that cause for which they gave the last full measure of devotion; that we here highly resolve that these dead shall not have died in vain; that this nation, under God, shall have a new birth of freedom; and that government of the people, by the people, for the people, shall not perish from the earth.

ABRAHAM LINCOLN: *Gettysburg Address*, 1865

3. Every thoughtful and unprejudiced mind must see that such an evil as slavery will yield only to the most radical treatment. If you consider the work we have to do, you will not think us needlessly aggressive, or that we dig down unnecessarily deep in laying the foundations of our enterprise. A money power of two thousand millions of dollars, as the prices of slaves now range, held by a small body of able and desperate men; that body raised into a political aristocracy by special constitutional provisions; cotton, the product of slave labor, forming the basis of our whole foreign commerce, and the commercial class thus subsidized; the press bought up, the pulpit reduced to vassalage, the heart of the common people chilled by a bitter prejudice against the black race; our leading men bribed, by ambition, either to silence or open hostility;—in such a land, on what shall an Abolitionist rely? On a few cold prayers, mere lip-service, and never from the heart? On a church resolution, hidden often in its records, and meant only as a decent cover for servility in daily practice? On political parties, with their superficial influence at best, and seeking ordinarily only to use existing prejudices to the best advantage? Slavery has deeper root here than any aristocratic institution has in Europe; and politics is but the common pulse-beat, of which revolution is the fever-spasm. Yet we have seen European aristocracy survive storms which seemed to reach down to the primal strata of European life. Shall we, then, trust to mere politics, where even revolution has failed? How shall the stream rise above its fountain? Where shall our church organizations or parties get strength to attack their great parent and moulder, the slave power? Shall the thing formed say to him that formed it, Why hastthou made me thus? The old jest of one who tried to lift himself in his own basket, is but a tame picture of the man who imagines that, by working solely through existing sects and parties, he can destroy slavery. Mechanics say nothing, but an earthquake strong enough to move all Egypt can bring down the pyramids.

Experience has confirmed these views. The Abolitionists who have acted on them have a "short method" with all unbelievers. They have but to point to their own success, in contrast with every other man's failure. To waken the nation to its real state, and chain it to the consideration of this one duty, is half the work. So much have we done. Slavery has been made the question of this generation. To startle the South to madness, so that every step she takes, in her blindness, is one step more toward ruin, is much. This we have done. Witness Texas and the Fugitive Slave Law.

WENDELL PHILLIPS: *The Abolition Movement*, 1853

4. Until just a few years ago flying was popularly regarded as a dangerous hobby and comparatively few had faith in its practical purposes. But the phenomenal evolutions of the aircraft industry during the war brought progress which would otherwise have required a span of years. With the cessation of hostilities considerable attention has been diverted to the commercial uses of aircraft, which may conveniently be classified as mail- and passenger-service.

Men who first ventured the prediction that postal and express matter would one day be carried through the air were branded as dreamers. Parts of that dream became a reality during 1918, and a more extensive aerial-mail program will be adopted this year. The dispatch with which important communications and parcels are delivered between large cities has firmly established its need.

Large passenger-carrying aircraft are now receiving pronounced attention. Lately developed by the Navy is a flying-boat having a wing area of 2,400 square feet, equipped with three Liberty motors and weighing 22,000 pounds with a full load. It is the largest seaplane in the world, and on a recent test-trip from Virginia to New York carried fifty-one passengers. At the present moment the public is awaiting the thrilling details of the first flight between Europe and America, which has just occurred as a result of the keen international rivalry involved between the various entrants.

The British are now constructing a super-triplane fitted with six 500 horse-power engines. Originally intended to carry 10,000 pounds of bombs and a crew of eight over a distance of 1,200 miles, the converted machine is

1

claimed to be able to carry approximately one hundred passengers. It has a wing span of 141 feet and a fuselage length of 85 feet.

What about the power plants of the future aircraft? Will the internal-combustion engine continue to reign supreme, or will increasing power demands of the huge planes to come lead to the development of suitable steam-engines? Will the use of petroleum continue to be one of the triumphs of aviation, or will the time come when substitutes may be successfully utilized?

For aerial motive-power, the principal requirements are: great power for weight with a fairly high factor of safety, compactness, reliability of operation under flying conditions, and safety from fire. Bulk and weight of steam-driven equipment apparently impose severe restrictions upon its practical development for present aircraft purposes, but who is willing to classify its future use as an absurdity?

Steam operation in small model airplanes is no innovation. Langley, in 1891-1895, built four model airplanes, one driven by carbonic-acid gas and three by steam-engines. One of the steam-driven models weighed thirty pounds, and on one occasion flew a distance of about three thousand feet. In 1913 an Englishman constructed a power plant weighing about two pounds which consisted of a flash boiler and single-acting engine. This unit employed benzolin, impure benzine, as fuel, and propelled a model plane weighing five pounds.

Power Plant Engineering, Chicago, June 1, 1919

Making a Brief. The next step after making outlines or briefs of material already organized is to make your own from material you gather. Speeches you have already prepared or considered as fit for presentation will supply you with ideas if you cannot work up new material in a short time. At first you will be more concerned with the form than the meaning of the entries, but even from the first you should consider the facts or opinions for which each topic or statement stands. Weigh its importance in the general scheme of details. Consider carefully its suitability for the audience who may be supposed to hear the finished speech. Discard the inappropriate. Replace the weak. Improve the indefinite. Be sure your examples and illustrations are apt.

Be wary about statistics. In listening to an address many people begin to distrust as soon as figures are mentioned. Statistics will illustrate and prove assertions, but they must be used judiciously. Do not use too many statistics. Never be too detailed. In a speech, $4,000,000 sounds more impressive than $4,232,196.96. Use round numbers. Never let them stand alone. Show their relationship. Burke quotes exact amounts to show the growth of the commerce of Pennsylvania, but he adds that it had increased fifty fold. A hearer will forget the numbers; he will remember the fact.

Similar reasons will warn you concerning the use of too many dates. They can be easily avoided by showing lapses of time—by saying, "fifty years later," or "when he was forty-six years old," or "this condition was endured only a score of months."

The chapters on introductions, conclusions, and planning material will have suggested certain orders for your briefs. Glance back at them for hints before you attempt to make the general scheme. Let two factors determine your resultant development—the nature of the material itself and the effect you want to produce.

In argumentative speeches a usual, as well as excellent, order is this:

1. Origin of the question. The immediate cause for discussion.

2. History of the question.

3. Definition of terms.

4. Main arguments.

5. Conclusion.

Why is the proposition worth discussing at this present time? Why do you choose it? Why is it timely? What is its importance? Why is a settlement needed? Any of these would fall under the first heading.

Has the matter engaged attention prior to the present? Has it changed? Was any settlement ever attempted? What was its result?

Are any of the words and phrases used likely to be misunderstood? Are any used in special senses? Do all people accept the same meaning? Good illustrations of this last are the ideas attached to *socialism, anarchist, soviet, union*.

To illustrate: the question of woman suffrage was brought into public interest once more by the advance woman has made in all walks of life and by the needs and lessons of the great war. To make clear how its importance had increased a speaker might trace its history from its first inception. As applied to women, what does "suffrage" mean exactly—the right to vote in all elections, or only in certain ones? Does it carry with it the right to hold office? Would the voting qualifications be the same for women as for men? Then would follow the arguments.

How could this scheme be used for a discussion of the Monroe Doctrine? For higher education? For education for girls? For child working laws? For a league of nations? For admitting Asiatic laborers to the United States? For advocating the study of the sciences? For urging men to become farmers? For predicting aerial passenger service? For a scholarship qualification in athletics? For abolishing railroad grade crossings? For equal wages for men and women?

EXERCISES

Make the completed brief for one or more of the preceding.

Briefs should be made for propositions selected from the following list.

1. The President of the United States should be elected by the direct vote of the people.

2. The States should limit the right of suffrage to persons who can read and write.

3. The President of the United States should be elected for a term of seven years, and be ineligible to reëlection.

4. A great nation should be made the mandatory over an inferior people.

5. Students should be allowed school credit for outside reading in connection with assigned work, or for editing of school papers, or for

participation in dramatic performances.

6. This state should adopt the "short ballot."

7. The present rules of football are unsatisfactory.

8. Coaching from the bench should be forbidden in baseball.

9. Compulsory military drill should be introduced into all educational institutions.

10. Participation in athletics lowers the scholarship of students.

11. Pupils should receive credit in school for music lessons outside.

12. The United States should abandon the Monroe Doctrine.

13. In jury trials, a three-fourths vote should be enough for the rendering of a verdict.

14. Strikes are unprofitable.

15. Commercial courses should be offered in all high schools.

16. Employers of children under sixteen should be required to provide at least eight hours of instruction a week for them.

17. Current events should be studied in all history or civics courses.

18. The practice of Christmas giving should be discontinued.

19. School buildings should be used as social centers.

20. Bring to class an editorial and an outline of it. Put the outline upon the board, or read it to the class. Then read the editorial.

Speaking from the Brief. Now that the brief is finished so that it represents exactly the material and development of the final speech, how shall it be used? To use it as the basis of a written article to be memorized is one method. Many speakers have employed such a method, many today do. The drawbacks of such memorizing have already been hinted at in an early chapter. If you want to grow in mental grasp, alertness, and power as a result of your speech training avoid this method. No matter how halting your first attempts may be, do not get into the seemingly easy, yet retarding habit of committing to memory. Memorizing has a decided value, but for speech-making the memory should be trained for larger matters than verbal reproduction. It should be used for the retention of facts while the other brain faculties are engaged in manipulating them for the best effect and finding words to express them forcefully. Memory is a helpful faculty. It should be cultivated in connection with the powers of understanding and expression, but it is not economical to commit a speech verbatim for delivery. The remarks will lack flexibility, spontaneity, and often direct appeal. There is a detached, mechanical air about a memorized speech which helps to ruin it.

With the outline before you, go over it carefully and slowly, mentally putting into words and sentences the entries you have inserted. You may even speak it half aloud to yourself, if that fixes the treatment more firmly in your mind. Then place the brief where you can reach it with your eye, and speak upon your feet. Some teachers recommend doing this before a mirror, but this is not always any help, unless you are conscious of awkward poses or gestures or movements, or facial contortions. Say the speech over thus, not only once but several times, improving the phraseology each time, changing where convenient or necessary, the emphasis, the amount of time, for each portion.

Self-criticism. Try to criticize yourself. This is not easy at first, but if you are consistent and persistent in your efforts you will be able to judge yourself in many respects. If you can induce some friend whose opinion is worth receiving either to listen to your delivery or to talk the whole thing over with you, you will gain much. In conference with the teacher before your delivery of the speech such help will be given. As you work over your brief in this manner you will be delighted to discover suddenly that you need refer to it less and less frequently. Finally, the outline will be in your mind, and when you speak you can give your entire attention to the delivery and the audience.

Do not be discouraged if you cannot retain all the outline the first times you try this method. Many a speaker has announced in his introduction, "I shall present four reasons," and often has sat down after discussing only three. Until you can dispense entirely with the brief keep it near you. Speak from it if you need it. Portions which you want to quote exactly (such as quotations from authorities) may be memorized or read. In reading be sure you read remarkably well. Few people can read interestingly before a large audience. Keep your papers where you can get at them easily. Be careful not to lose your place so that you will have to shuffle them to get the cue for continuing. Pauses are not dangerous when they are made deliberately for effect, but they are ruinous when they betray to the audience forgetfulness or embarrassment on the part of the speaker. Anticipate your need. Get your help before you actually need it, so that you can continue gracefully.

Results. This method, followed for a few months, will develop speaking ability. It produces results suited to modern conditions of all kinds of life. It develops practically all the mental faculties and personal attributes. It puts the speaker directly in touch with his audience. It permits him to adapt his material to an occasion and audience. It gives him the opportunity to sway his hearers and used legitimately for worthy ends, this is the most worthy purpose of any speech.

1

CHAPTER IX

EXPLAINING

The part which explanation plays in all phases of life is too apparent to need any emphasis here. It is to a great extent the basis of all our daily intercourse, from explaining to a teacher why a lesson has not been prepared, to painstakingly explaining to a merchant why a bill has not been paid. An instructor patiently explains a problem to a class, and a merchant explains the merits of an article or the operation of a device to his customers. The politician explains why he should be elected. The financier explains the returns from stock and bond purchases. The President explains to the Senate the reason for treaty clauses. The minister explains the teachings of his faith to his congregation. You can make this list as long as the varied activities of all life.

Exposition. This kind of discourse, the purpose of which is explanation, is also called exposition. Has it any relation to the underlying idea of the term *exposition* as applied to a great exhibition or fair? Its purpose is plainly information, the transmission of knowledge. While description and narration exist primarily to entertain, exposition exists to convey information. Description and narration may be classed as literature of entertainment; exposition as literature of knowledge. It answers such questions as how? why? for what purpose? in what manner? by what method? It can sometimes be used to convince a person with opposing views, for frequently you hear a man to whom the explanation of a belief has been made, exclaim, "Oh, if that's what you mean, I agree with you entirely." All instruction, all directions of work, all scientific literature, are in foundation expository. In its simplest, most disconnected form, exposition gives its value to that most essential volume, the dictionary.

Make a list of other kinds of books which are mainly or entirely expository in character.

Difficulties in Exposition. Such are the purpose and use of exposition. The difficulty of producing good exposition is evident from those two factors. As it, exists everywhere, as it purposes to inform, its first requisite is clearness. Without that quality it is as nothing. When you direct a stranger how to reach a certain building in your town, of what value are your remarks unless they are clear? When a scientist writes a treatise on the topic of the immortality of man, of what value are his opinions unless his statements are clear? All the other qualities which prose may and should possess sink into subordinate value in exposition when compared with clearness. Because of all three phases of exposition—its universal use, its informative purpose, its essential clarity—exposition is an all-important topic for the consideration and practice of the public speaker. In its demand for clearness lies also its difficulty. Is it easy to tell the exact truth, not as a moral exercise, but merely as a matter of exactness? Why do the careless talkers speak so often of "a sort of pink" or "a kind of revolving shaft" or tack on at the end of phrases the meaningless "something" or "everything" except that even in their unthinking minds there is the hazy impression—they really never have a well-defined idea—that they have not said exactly what they want to say?

Clear Understanding. Here then is the first requisite for the public speaker. He must have no hazy impressions, no unthinking mind, no ill-defined ideas, no inexactness. He must have a clear understanding of all he tries to tell to others. Without this the words of a speaker are as sounding brass and tinkling cymbals. Or he may deliver a great roar of words signifying nothing. This is the fault with most recitations of pupils in school—they do not get a clear understanding of the material assigned to them for mastery. As a test of the degree of understanding, the recitation method serves admirably. The lecture method of instruction—clear though the presentation may be—offers no manner of finding out, until the final examination, how much the pupil actually understands. So far, in public speaking, the only way of learning that the student understands the principles and can apply them is to have him speak frequently to indicate his ability. Can you not name among your associates and friends those whose explanations are lucid, concise, direct, unconfusing, and others whose attempts at exposition are jumbled, verbose, unenlightening?

Have you not criticized certain teachers by remarking "they may know their own subjects all right, but they couldn't impart their knowledge to the class"?

Command of Language. What was lacking in their case? Certainly, to be charitable, we cannot say they lacked a clear understanding of their own topic. It must have been something else. That second element, which is at times almost entirely absent when the first is present, is the command of language. Many a man knows a great deal but is incapable of transmitting his knowledge. He lacks the gift of expression. He has not cultivated it—for it can be cultivated. The man whose desire or vocation forces him to make the effort to speak will train himself in methods of communication, until he arrives at comfort and fluency.

The district manager of a large electric company related that as he would sit at a meeting of the directors or committee of a large corporation and realized that the moment was approaching when he would be called upon to speak he would feel his senses grow confused, a sinking feeling amounting almost to faintness would sweep over him. Strong in his determination to do the best he could for his company he would steady his nerves by saying to himself, "You know more about this matter than any of these men. That's why you are here. Tell them what you know so plainly that they will understand as well as you do." There was, you see, the reassurance of complete understanding of the subject coupled with the endeavor to express it clearly. These two elements, then, are of supreme significance to the public speaker. Even to the person who desires to write well, they are all-important. To the speaker they are omnipresent. The effect of these two upon the intellectual development is marked. The desire for clear understanding will keep the mind stored with material to assimilate and communicate. It will induce the mind continually to manipulate this material to secure clarity in presentation. This will result in developing a mental adroitness of inestimable value to the speaker, enabling him to seize the best method instantaneously and apply it to his purposes. At the same time, keeping always in view the use of this material as the basis of communicating information or convincing by making explanations, he will be solicitous about his language. Words will take on new values. He will be continually searching for new ones to express the exact differences of ideas he wants to convey. He will try different expressions, various phrases, changed word orders, to test their efficacy and appropriateness in transferring his meaning to his hearers. Suggestions offered in the chapter of this book on words and sentences will never cease to operate in his thinking and speaking. There will be a direct result in his ability as a speaker and a reflex result upon his ability as a thinker. What is more encouraging, he will realize and appreciate these results himself, and his satisfaction in doing better work will be doubled by the delight in knowing exactly how he secured the ends for which he strove.

Methods of Explaining. In order to make a matter clear, to convey information, a speaker has at his disposal many helpful ways of arranging his material. Not all topics can be treated in all or even any certain one of the following manners, but if the student is familiar with certain processes he will the more easily and surely choose just that one suited to the topic he intends to explain and the circumstances of his exposition.

Division. One of these methods is by division. A speaker may separate a topic or term into the parts which comprise it. For instance, a scientist may have to list all the kinds of electricity; a Red Cross instructor may divide all bandages into their several kinds; an athletic coach may have to explain all the branches of sports in order to induce more candidates to appear for certain events; a banker may have to divide financial operations to make clear an advertising pamphlet soliciting new lines of business, such as drawing up of wills.

The ability to do this is a valuable mental accomplishment as well as an aid to speaking. In dividing, care must be taken to make the separations according to one principle for any one class. It would not result in clearness to divide all men according to height, and at the same time according to color. This would result in confusion. Divide according to height first, then divide the classes so formed according to color if needed—as might be done in military formation. Each group, then, must be distinctly marked off from all other groups. In scientific and technical matters such division may be carried to the extreme limit of completeness. Complete division is called classification.

Partition. In non-scientific compositions such completeness is seldom necessary. It might even defeat the purpose by being too involved, by including too many entries, and by becoming difficult to remember. Speakers seldom have need of classification, but they often do have to make divisions for purposes of explanation. This kind of grouping is called partition. It goes only so far as is necessary for the purpose at the time. It may stop anywhere short of being complete and scientifically exact. All members of the large class not divided and listed are frequently lumped together under a last heading such as *all others, miscellaneous, the rest, those not falling under our present examination.*

EXERCISES

1. Classify games. Which principle will you use for your first main division —indoor and outdoor games, or winter and summer games, or some other?

2. Classify the races of men. What principle would you use?

3. How would you arrange the books in a private library?

4. Classify the forms of theatrical entertainments. Is your list complete?

5. Classify branches of mathematics. The entries may total over a hundred.

6. Classify the pupils in your school.

7. Classify the people in your school. Is there any difference?

8. Classify the following:

> The political parties of the country.
> Methods of transportation.
> Religions.
> Magazines.
> The buildings in a city.
> Aircraft.
> Desserts.
> Canned goods.

Skill in division is valuable not only as a method of exposition but it is linked closely with an effective method of proving to be explained in the next chapter—the method of residues. Can you recall any extracts given in this book in which some form of division is used? Is this form of material likely to be more important in preparation or in the finished speech? Explain your opinion—in other words, present a specimen of exposition.

Definition. One of the simplest ways of explaining is to define a term. Dictionary definitions are familiar to everyone. In a great many instances the dictionary definition is by means of synonyms. While this is a convenient, easy method it is seldom exact. Why? Recall what you learned concerning the meanings of synonyms. Do they ever exactly reproduce one another's meanings? There is always a slight degree of inaccuracy in definition by synonym, sometimes a large margin of inexactness. Is the following a good definition?

A visitor to a school began his address: "This morning, children, I propose to offer you an epitome of the life of St. Paul. It may be perhaps that there are among you some too young to grasp the meaning of the word *epitome*. *Epitome*, children, is in its signification synonymous with synopsis!"

London Tid-Bits

Logical Definition. An exact definition is supplied by the logical definition. In this there are three parts—the term to be defined, the class (or genus) to which it belongs, and the distinguishing characteristics (differentia) which mark it off from all the other members of that same class. You can represent this graphically by inclosing the word *term* in a small circle. Around this draw a larger circle in which you write the word *class*. Now what divides the term from the class in which it belongs? Indicate the line around the *term* as *distinguishing characteristics*, and you will clearly see how accurate a logical definition is. The class should be just larger than the term itself. The main difficulty is in finding exact and satisfying distinguishing characteristics. There are some terms which are so large that no classes can be found for them. Others cannot be marked by acceptable distinguishing characteristics, so it is not possible to make logical definitions for all terms. Consider such words as *infinity, electricity, gravity, man.*

The words of the definition should be simple, more readily understood than the term to be defined.

Term	Class	Distinguishing characteristics
A biplane	is an airplane	with two sets of supporting surfaces.
A waitress	is a woman	who serves meals.
Narration	is that form of discourse	which relates events.
A word	is a combination	suggesting an idea.

A dictionary	is a book	of letters of definitions.
A corporal	is an army officer	just higher than a private.

EXERCISES

1. Make logical definitions for the following:

A dynamo	A circle	A hammer
A curiosity	Lightning	A trip-hammer
Moving picture camera	Democracy	A lady
Curiosity	An anarchist	A Lady
A door	A sky-scraper	Man

2. Analyze and comment on the following definitions:

Man is a two-legged animal without feathers.

Life is an epileptic fit between two nothings.

Genius is an infinite capacity for taking pains.

The picture writings of the ancient Egyptians are called hieroglyphics.

A fly is an obnoxious insect that disturbs you in the morning when you want to sleep.

Real bravery is defeated cowardice.

A brigantine is a small, two-masted vessel, square rigged on both masts, but with a fore-and-aft mainsail and the mainmast considerably longer than the foremast.

A mushroom is a cryptogamic plant of the class *Fungi*; particularly the agaricoid fungi and especially the edible forms.

Language is the means of concealing thought.

A rectangle of equal sides is a square.

Hyperbole is a natural exaggeration for the purpose of emphasis.

Amplified Definition. While such definitions are the first positions from which all interpretations must proceed, in actual speech-making explanations of terms are considerably longer. Yet the form of the true logical definition is always imbedded—in germ at least—in the amplified statement.

> Again, democracy will be, in a large sense, individualistic. That ideal of society which seeks a disciplined, obedient people, submissive to government and unquestioning in its acceptance of orders, is not a democratic ideal. You cannot have an atmosphere of "implicit obedience to authority" and at the same time and in the same place an atmosphere of democratic freedom. There is only one kind of discipline that is adequate to democracy and that is self-discipline. An observant foreigner has lately remarked, somewhat paradoxically, that the Americans seemed to him the best disciplined people in the world. In no other country does a line form itself at a ticket office or at the entrance to a place of amusement with so little disorder, so little delay, and so little help from a policeman. In no other country would an appeal of the government for self-control in the use of food or fuel, for a restriction of hours of business, for "gas-less Sundays," have met with so ready, so generous and so sufficient a response. Our American lads, alert, adaptable, swiftly-trained, self-directed, have been quite the equal of the continental soldiers, with their longer technical training and more rigorous military discipline. In these respects the English, and especially the British colonial soldiers have been much like our own. Democracy, whether for peace or for war, in America or in England, favors individuality. Independence of thought and action on the part of the mass of the people are alike the result of democracy and the condition of its continuance and more complete development, and it is visibly growing in England as the trammels of old political and social class control are being thrown off.

What is a constitution? Certainly not a league, compact, or confederacy, but a fundamental law. That fundamental regulation which determines the manner in which the public authority is to be executed, is what forms the constitution of a state. Those primary rules which concern the body itself, and the very being of the political society, the form of government, and the manner in which power is to be exercised—all, in a word, which form together the constitution of a state—these are the fundamental laws. This, Sir, is the language of the public writers. But do we need to be informed, in this country, what a constitution is? Is it not an idea perfectly familiar, definite, and well settled? We are at no loss to understand what is meant by the constitution of one of the States; and the Constitution of the United States speaks of itself as being an instrument of the same nature.

Daniel Webster: *The Constitution Not a Compact between Sovereign States*, 1833

Particulars of a General Statement. A general statement made at the beginning of a paragraph or section, serving as the topic sentence, may then be explained by breaking the general idea up into details and particulars. This may partake of the nature of both definition and partition, as the terms may be explained and their component parts listed. Note that in the following selection the first sentences state the topic of the passage which the succeeding sentences explain by discussing the phrase *variety of evils*.

So likewise a passionate attachment of one nation for another produces a variety of evils. Sympathy for the favorite nation, facilitating the illusion of an imaginary common interest, in cases where no real common interest exists, and infusing into one the enmities of the other, betrays the former into a participation in the quarrels and wars of the latter, without adequate inducement or justification. It leads also to concessions to the favorite nation of privileges denied to others, which is apt doubly to injure the nation making the concessions; by unnecessarily parting with what ought to have been retained, and by exciting jealousy, ill-will, and a disposition to retaliate, in the parties from whom equal privileges are withheld, and it gives to ambitious, corrupted, or deluded citizens (who devote themselves to the favorite nation), facility to betray, or sacrifice the interests of their own country, without odium, sometimes even with popularity; gilding with the appearances of a virtuous sense of obligation, a commendable deference for public opinion, or a laudable zeal for public good, the base or foolish compliances of ambition, corruption or infatuation.

GEORGE WASHINGTON: *Farewell Address*, 1796

Examples. A statement may be explained by giving examples. The speaker must be sure that his example fits the case exactly; that it is typical—that is, it must serve as a true instance of all cases under the statement, not be merely an exception; that it is perfectly clear; that it impresses the audience as unanswerable. The example may be either actual or suppositious, but it must illustrate clearly and accurately. The use of examples is a great aid in explanation. John C. Calhoun expressed the value very distinctly in one of his speeches.

> I know how difficult it is to communicate distinct ideas on such a subject, through the medium of general propositions, without particular illustration; and in order that I may be distinctly understood, though at the hazard of being tedious, I will illustrate the important principle which I have ventured to advance, by examples.

By the use of an example he does make himself distinctly understood.

> Let us, then, suppose a small community of five persons, separated from the rest of the world; and, to make the example strong, let us suppose them all to be engaged in the same pursuit, and to be of equal wealth. Let us further suppose that they determine to govern the community by the will of a majority; and, to make the case as strong as possible, let us suppose that the majority, in order to meet the expenses of the government, lay an equal tax, say of one hundred dollars on

each individual of this little community. Their treasury would contain five hundred dollars. Three are a majority; and they, by supposition, have contributed three hundred as their portion, and the other two (the minority), two hundred. The three have the right to make the appropriations as they may think proper. The question is, How would the principle of the absolute and unchecked majority operate, under these circumstances, in this little community?

JOHN C. CALHOUN: *Speech on The Force Bill*, 1833

The example should be taken from the same phase of life as the proposition it explains. As Calhoun was discussing governmental regulation he supposed an example from majority rule. In the next the topic is copyright, so the illustration is not taken from patents. In introducing your own examples avoid the trite, amateurish expression "take, for instance."

Now, this is the sort of boon which my honorable and learned friend holds out to authors. Considered as a boon to them, it is a mere nullity; but, considered as an impost on the public, it is no nullity, but a very serious and pernicious reality. I will take an example. Dr. Johnson died fifty-six years ago. If the law were what my honorable and learned friend wishes to make it, somebody would now have the monopoly of Dr. Johnson's works. Who that somebody would be it is impossible to say; but we may venture to guess. I guess, then, that it would have been some bookseller, who was the assign of another bookseller, who was the grandson of a third bookseller, who had bought the copyright from Black Frank, the doctor's servant and residuary legatee, in 1785 or 1786. Now, would the knowledge that this copyright would exist in 1841 have been a source of gratification to Johnson? Would it have stimulated his exertions? Would it have once drawn him out of his bed before noon? Would it have once cheered him under a fit of the spleen? Would it have induced him to give us one more allegory, one more life of a poet, one more imitation of Juvenal? I firmly believe not. I firmly believe that a hundred years ago, when he was writing our debates for the *Gentleman's Magazine*, he would very much rather have had twopence to buy a plate of shin of beef at a cook's shop underground.

Thomas Babington Macaulay: *Copyright*, 1841

Comparison. Unfamiliar matter may be made plain by showing how it resembles something already clearly understood by the audience. This is comparison. It shows how two things are alike. The old geographies used to state that the earth is an oblate spheroid, then explain that term by comparison with an orange, pointing out the essential flattening at the poles. In any use of comparison the resemblance must be real, not assumed. Many a speaker has been severely criticized for his facts because he asserted in comparison similarities that did not exist.

Contrast. When the *differences* between two things are carefully enumerated the process is termed contrast. This is often used in combination with comparison, for no two things are exactly alike. They may resemble each other in nearly all respects, so comparison is possible and helpful up to a certain limit. To give an exact idea of the remainder the differences must be pointed out; that requires contrast.

In contrast the opposing balance of details does not have to depend necessarily on a standard familiar to the audience. It may be an arrangement of opposite aspects of the same thing to bring out more vividly the understanding. In his *History of the English People*, Green explains the character of Queen Elizabeth by showing the contrasted elements she inherited from her mother, Anne Boleyn, and her father, Henry VIII. Such a method results not only in added clearness, but also in emphasis. The plan may call for half a paragraph on one side, the second half on the other; or it may cover two paragraphs or sections; or it may alternate with every detail —an affirmative balanced by a negative, followed at once by another pair of affirmative and negative, or statement and contrast, and so on until the end. The speaker must consider such possibilities of contrast, plan for his own, and indicate it in his brief.

Nearly any speech will provide illustrations of the methods of comparison and contrast. Burke's *Conciliation with America* has several passages of each.

Cause to Effect. Explanations based on progressions from cause to effect and the reverse are admirably suited to operations, movements, changes, conditions, elections. An exposition of a manufacturing process might move from cause to effect. A legislator trying to secure the passage of a measure might explain its operation by beginning with the law (the cause) and tracing its results (the effect). So, too, a reformer might plead for a changed condition by following the same method. A speaker dealing with history or biography might use this same plan.

Effect to Cause. In actual events, the cause always precedes the effect, but in discussion it is sometimes better not to follow natural or usual orders. Many explanations gain in clearness and effect by working backwards. A voter might begin by showing the condition of a set of workmen (an effect), then trace conditions backward until he would end with a plea for the repeal of a law (the cause). A student might explain a low mark on his report by starting with the grading (the effect) and tracing backwards all his struggles to an early absence by which he missed a necessary explanation by the teacher. A doctor might begin a report by stating the illness of several persons with typhus; then trace preceding conditions step by step until he reached the cause—oysters eaten by them in a hotel were kept cool by a dealer's letting water run over them. This water in its course had picked up the disease germs—the cause. Many crimes are solved by moving from effect to cause. A lawyer in his speeches, therefore, frequently follows this method.

Both these methods are so commonly employed that the student can cite instances from many speeches he has heard or books he has read.

Time Order. Somewhat similar to the two preceding arrangements of exposition are the next two based on time. The first of these is the natural time order, or chronological order. In this the details follow one another as events happened. It is to be noted, however, that not any group of succeeding details will make a good exposition of this sort. The parts must be closely related. They must be not merely *sequential* but *consequential*. Dictionary definitions will explain the difference in meaning of those two words. This method is somewhat like the order from cause to effect, but it is adapted to other kinds of topics and other purposes of explanation. It is excellently suited to historical material, or any related kind. It is the device

1

usually employed in explaining mechanical or manufacturing processes. In mere frequency of occurrence it is doubtlessly the most common.

Time Order Reversed. The student who starts to cast his expositions into this scheme should judge its fitness for his particular purpose at the time. It will often become apparent upon thought that instead of the natural chronological order the exact opposite will suit better. This—time order reversed—explains itself as the arrangement from the latest occurrence back through preceding events and details until the earliest time is reached. It is quite like the arrangement from effect back to cause. It might be used to explain the legal procedure of a state or nation, to explain treaty relations, to explain the giving up of old laws. The movements of a man accused of crime might be explained in this way. An alibi for a person might be built up thus. The various versions of some popular story told over and over again through a long period of years might be explained after such a manner.

Although the time order reversed is not so common as the chronological order it does occur many times.

Place. Certain material of exposition demands the order of place. This means that the details of the explanation are arranged according to the position of objects. If you have written many descriptions you are familiar with the problems brought up by such an order. A few illustrations will make it clear. A man on the street asks you how to reach a certain point in the city. On what plan do you arrange your directions? According to their place? You start to explain to a friend the general lay-out of New York, or Chicago, or San Francisco. How do you arrange the details of your exposition? You attempt to convey to another person the plan of some large building. What arrangement is inevitable? How do books on sports explain the baseball field, the football gridiron, the tennis court, the golf links? When specifications for a building are furnished to the contractor, what principle of arrangement is followed? If an inventor gives instructions to a pattern-maker for the construction of a model, what plan does he follow? Would a man discussing drawings for a new house be likely to formulate his explanations on this scheme?

You see, then, how well suited such an arrangement is to a variety of uses. In such expository passages the transition and connecting words are mainly expressions of place and relative position such as *to the right, above, below, to the rear, extending upwards at an angle of sixty degrees, dividing equally into three sections.* Such indications must never be slighted in spoken explanations. They keep the material clear and exact in the hearer's comprehension. The speaker, remember, can never assume that his audience is bound to understand him. His task is to be so clear that no single individual can fail to understand him.

Importance. It has already been stated—in the chapter on planning—that topics may be arranged in the order of their importance. This same scheme may be used in delivery of expository matter. A hearer will follow the explanation if he be led gradually up the ascent; he will remember most clearly the latter part of the passage. If this include the prime factor of the information he will retain it longest and most clearly. You should listen to speeches of explanations critically to judge whether the plans are good. Should you make a list of the number of times any of the plans here set down appears you will be struck by the fact that while other orders are quite frequent, this last principle of leading up to the most important outranks all the others. It may be simply a form of one of the others previously enumerated in which time order, or contrast, or cause to effect is followed simply because that does bring the most important last in the discussion. Such an arrangement answers best to the response made to ideas by people in audiences. It is a principle of all attempts to instruct them, to appeal to them, to stimulate them, to move them, that the successive steps must increase in significance and impressiveness until the most moving details be laid before them. Analyze for yourself or for the class a few long explanations you have listened to, and report whether this principle was followed. Does it bear any relation to concluding a speech with a peroration?

Combinations of Methods. While any one of the foregoing methods may be used for a single passage it is not usual in actual practice to find one scheme used throughout all the explanatory matter of the speech. In the first place, the attention of the audience would very likely become wearied by the monotony of such a device. Certain parts of the material under explanation seem to require one treatment, other portions require different handling. Therefore good speakers usually combine two or more of these plans.

Partition could hardly be used throughout an entire speech without ruining its interest. It occurs usually early to map out the general field or scope. Definition also is likely to be necessary at the beginning of an explanation to start the audience with clear ideas. It may be resorted to at various times later whenever a new term is introduced with a meaning the audience may not entirely understand. Both partition and definition are short, so they are combined with other forms. Examples, likewise, may be introduced anywhere.

The two most frequently closely combined are comparison and contrast. Each seems to require the other. Having shown how two things or ideas are alike, the speaker naturally passes on to secure more definiteness by showing that with all their likenesses they are not exactly the same, and that the differences are as essential to a clear comprehension of them as the similarities. So usual are they that many people accept the two words as meaning almost the same thing, though in essence they are opposites.

The other orders cannot be used in such close combinations but they may be found in varying degrees in many extended speeches of explanation as the nature of the material lends itself to one treatment or another. A twelve-hundred word discussion of *The Future of Food* uses examples, contrasted examples, effect to cause, cause to effect (the phrase beginning a paragraph is "there is already evidence that this has resulted in a general lowering "), while the succeeding parts grow in significance until the last is the most important. A great English statesman in a speech lasting some three hours on a policy of government employed the following different methods at various places where he introduced expository material—partition (he claimed it was classification, but he listed for consideration only three of the essential five choices), contrast, comparison, time, example, place, cause to effect. Some of these methods of arranging explanatory matter were used several times.

EXERCISES

1. Explain a topic by giving three examples. The class should comment upon their value.

2. Explain to the class some mechanical operation or device. The class after listening should decide which method the speaker used.

3. Explain some principle of government or society following the time order.

4. With a similar topic follow time reversed.

5. With a similar topic use comparison only.

6. Follow an arrangement based on contrast only.

7. In explaining a topic combine comparison and contrast.

8. Explain some proverb, text, or quotation. The class should discuss the arrangement.

9. Choose some law or government regulation. Condemn or approve it in an explanation based on cause to effect.

10. With the same or a similar topic use effect to cause.

11. Explain to the class the plan of some large building or group of buildings. Is your explanation easily understood?

12. Explain why a certain study fits one for a particular vocation. Use the order of importance.

13. Give an idea of two different magazines, using comparison and contrast.

14. Explain some game. Time order?

15. How is a jury trial conducted?

16. Explain the principles of some political party.

17. Speak for four minutes upon exercise in a gymnasium.

18. Tell how a school paper, or daily newspaper, or magazine is conducted.

19. What is slang?

20. Explain one of your hobbies.

21. Classify and explain the qualities of a good speaker. Order of importance?

22. Explain some natural phenomenon.

23. Explain the best method for studying.

24. Contrast business methods.

25. From some business (as stock selling) or industry (as automobile manufacturing) or new vocation (as airplaning) or art (as acting) or accomplishment (as cooking) choose a group of special terms and explain them in a connected series of remarks.

26. Why is superstition so prevalent? The class should discuss the explanations presented.

27. "The point that always perplexes me is this: I always feel that if all the wealth was shared out, it would be all the same again in a few years' time. No one has ever explained to me how you can get over that." Explain clearly one of the two views suggested here.

28. Explain the failure of some political movement, or the defeat of some nation.

29. Select a passage from some book, report, or article, couched in intricate technical or specialized phraseology. Explain it clearly to the class.

30. Ben Jonson, a friend of Shakespeare's, wrote of him, "He was not of an age, but for all time." What did he mean?

CHAPTER X

PROVING AND PERSUADING

What Argumentation Is. It is an old saying that there are two sides to every question. Any speaker who supports some opinion before an audience, who advances some theory, who urges people to do a certain thing, to vote a certain way, to give money for charitable purposes, recognizes the opposite side. In trying to make people believe as he believes, to induce them to act as he advises, he must argue with them. Argumentation, as used in this book, differs widely from the informal exchange of opinions and views indulged in across the dinner table or on the trolley car. It does not correspond with the usual meaning of argue and argument which both so frequently suggest wrangling and bickering ending in ill-tempered personal attacks. Argumentation is the well-considered, deliberate means employed to convince others of the truth or expediency of the views advocated by the speaker. Its purpose is to carry conviction to the consciousness of others. This is its purpose. Its method is proof. Proof is the body of facts, opinions, reasons, illustrations, conclusions, etc., properly arranged and effectively presented which makes others accept as true or right the proposition advanced by the speaker. Of course, argumentation may exist in writing but as this volume is concerned with oral delivery, the word speaker is used in the definition. So much for the purpose and nature of argumentation.

Use of Argumentation. Where is it used? Everywhere, in every form of human activity. Argumentation is used by a youngster trying to induce a companion to go swimming and by a committee of world statesmen discussing the allotment of territory. In business a man uses it from the time he successfully convinces a firm it should employ him as an office boy until he secures the acceptance of his plans for a combination of interests which will control the world market. Lawyers, politicians, statesmen, clergymen, live by argumentation. In the life of today, which emphasizes so markedly the two ideas of individuality and efficiency, argumentation is of paramount importance.

Any person can argue, in the ordinary sense of stating opinions and views, in so far as any one can converse. But to produce good, convincing argumentation is not so easy as that. The expression of personal preferences, opinions, ideas, is not argumentation, although some people who advance so far as to become speakers before audiences seem never to realize that truth, and display themselves as pretending to offer argumentation when they are in reality doing no more than reciting personal beliefs and suggestions.

Cite instances of speakers who have indulged in such personal opinions when they might or should have offered arguments.

While argumentation is not so easily assembled as running conversation is, it may be made quite as fascinating as the latter, and just as surely as a person can have his conversational ability developed so can a person have his argumentative power strengthened.

Conviction. What should be the first requisite of a speaker of argumentation? Should it be conviction in the truth or right of the position he takes and the proposition he supports? At first thought one would answer emphatically "yes." A great deal of discredit has been brought upon the study of argumentation by the practice of speakers to pretend to have opinions which in reality they do not sincerely believe. The practical instance is the willingness of paid lawyers to defend men of whose guilt they must be sure. Such criticism does not apply to cases in which there are reasonable chances for opposing interpretations, nor to those cases in which our law decrees that every person accused of crime shall be provided with counsel, but to those practices to which Lincoln referred when he recommended the lawyer not to court litigation. Nor should this criticism deter a student of public speaking from trying his skill in defense of the other side, when he feels that such practice will help him in weighing his own arguments. In every instance of this highly commendable double method of preparation which the author has seen in classrooms, the speaker, after his speech has been commented upon, has always declared his real position and explained why he advocated the opposite. Even school and college debating has been criticized in the same way for becoming not an attempt to discover or establish the truth or right of a proposition, but a mere game with formal rules, a set of scoring regulations, and a victory or defeat with consequent good or bad effects upon the whole practice of undergraduate debating. If such contests are understood in their true significance, as practice in training, and the assumption of conviction by a student is not continued after graduation so that he will in real life defend and support opinions he really does not believe, the danger is not so great. The man who has no fixed principles, who can argue equally glibly on any side of a matter, whose talents are at any man's command of service, is untrustworthy. Convictions are worthy elements in life. A man must change his stand when his convictions are argued away, but the man whose opinions shift with every new scrap of information or influence is neither a safe leader nor a dependable subordinate.

For the sake of the training, then, a student *may* present arguments from attitudes other than his own sincere conviction, but the practice should be nothing more than a recognized exercise.

Because of its telling influence upon the opinion of others let us, without further reservation, set down that the first essential of a good argument is the ability to convince others. Aside from the language and the manner of delivery—two elements which must never be disregarded in any speech—this ability to convince others depends upon the proof presented to them in support of a proposition. The various kinds and methods of proof, with matters closely related to them, make up the material of this chapter.

The Proposition. In order to induce argument, there must be a proposition. A proposition in argument is a statement—a declarative sentence—concerning the truth or expediency of which there may be two opinions. Notice that not every declarative statement is a proposition for argument. "The sun rises" is not a statement about which there can be any varying opinions. It is not a proposition for argument. But "Missionaries should not be sent to China," and "John Doe killed Simon Lee," are statements admitting of different opinions and beliefs. They are propositions for argument. No sane person would argue about such a statement as "Missionaries are sent to China," nor would any one waste time on such a statement as "Some day a man named John Doe will kill a man named Simon Lee."

Although in common language we speak of arguing a question the student must remember that such a thing is impossible. You cannot argue about a question. Nor can you argue about a subject or a topic. The only expression about which there can be any argument is a proposition. The question must be answered. The resulting statement is then proved or disproved. The topic must be given some definite expression in a declarative sentence before any real argument is possible. Even when the matter of argument is incorrectly phrased as a topic or question you will find almost immediately in the remarks the proposition as a sentence. "Should women vote?" may be on the posters announcing an address, but the speaker will soon declare, "Women should vote in all elections in the United States upon the same conditions that men do." That is the proposition being argued; the question has been answered.

Kinds of Propositions. Certain kinds of propositions should never be chosen for argumentation. Many are incapable of proof, so any speech upon them would result in the mere repetition of personal opinions. Such are: The pen is mightier than the sword; Business men should not read poetry; Every person should play golf; Ancient authors were greater than modern authors. Others are of no interest to contemporary audiences and for that reason should not be presented. In the Middle Ages scholars discussed such matters as how many angels could stand on the point of a needle, but today no one cares about such things.

Propositions of Fact. Propositions fall into the two classes already illustrated by the statements about missionaries in China and the killing of Simon Lee. The second—John Doe killed Simon Lee—is a proposition of fact. All argument about it would tend to prove either the affirmative or the negative. One argument would strive to prove the statement a fact. The other argument would try to prove its opposite the actual fact. Facts are accomplished results or finished events. Therefore propositions of fact refer to the past. They are the material of argument in all cases at law, before investigation committees, and in similar proceedings. Lincoln argued a proposition of fact when he took Douglas's statement, "Our fathers, when they framed the government under which we live, understood this question just as well, and even better, than we do now," and then proved by telling exactly how they voted upon every measure dealing with slavery exactly what the thirty-nine signers of the Constitution did believe about national control of the practice. Courts of law demand that pleadings "shall set forth with certainty and with truth the matters of fact or of law, the truth or falsity of which must be decided to decide the case."

Propositions of Policy. Notice that the other proposition—Missionaries should not be sent to China—is not concerned with a fact at all. It deals with something which should or should not be done. It deals with future conduct. It depends upon the value of the results to be secured. It looks to the future. It deals with some principle of action. It is a question of expediency or policy. It induces argument to show that one method is the best or not the best. Propositions of expediency or policy are those which confront all of us at every step in life. Which college shall a boy attend? What kind of work shall a woman enter? How large shall taxes be next year? Which candidate shall we elect? How shall we better the city government? How shall I invest my money? What kind of automobile shall I buy? What kind of will shall I make?

The answers to all such questions make propositions of expediency or policy upon which arguments are being composed and delivered every day.

In choosing propositions for argument avoid, 1, those which are obviously truth; 2, those in which some ambiguous word or term covers the truth; 3, those in which the truth or error is practically impossible of proof; 4, those involving more than one main issue; 5, those which do not interest the audience.

Wording the Proposition. The proposition should be accurately worded. In law if the word *burglary* is used in the indictment, the defense, in order to quash the charge, need show merely that a door was unlocked. The phrasing should be as simple and concise as possible. The proposition should not cover too wide a field. Although these directions seem self-evident they should be kept in mind continually.

When the proposition is satisfactory to the maker of the argument he is ready to begin to build his proof. In actual speech-making few arguments can be made as convincing as a geometrical demonstration but a speaker can try to make his reasoning so sound, his development so cogent, his delivery so convincing, that at the end of his speech, he can exclaim triumphantly, "Quod erat demonstrandum."

Burden of Proof. Every argument presupposes the opposite side. Even when only one speaker appears his remarks always indicate the possibility of opposite views in the minds of some of the hearers. The affirmative and negative are always present. It is frequently asserted that the burden of proof is on the negative. This is no more correct than the opposite statement would be. The place of the burden of proof depends entirely upon the wording of the proposition and the statement it makes. In general the burden of proof is upon the side which proposes any change of existing conditions, the side which supports innovations, which would introduce new methods. With the passage of time the burden of proof may shift from one side to the other. There was a time when the burden of proof was upon the advocates of woman suffrage; today it is undoubtedly upon the opponents. At one period the opponents of the study of Latin and Greek had the burden of proof, now the supporters of such study have it. Other topics upon which the burden of proof has shifted are popular election of Senators, prohibition, League of Nations, self-determination of small nations, the study of vocations, civics, and current topics in schools, an all-year school term, higher salaries for teachers, the benefits of labor unions, Americanization of the foreign born.

Evidence. One of the best ways of proving a statement is by giving evidence of its truth. Evidence is made up of facts which support any proposition. In court a witness when giving testimony (evidence) is not allowed to give opinions or beliefs—he is continually warned to offer only what he knows of the fact. It is upon the facts marshaled before it that the jury is charged to render its verdict.

Direct Evidence. Evidence may be of two kinds—direct and indirect. This second, especially in legal matters, is termed circumstantial evidence. Direct evidence consists of facts that apply directly to the proposition under consideration. If a man sees a street car passenger take a wallet from another man's pocket and has him arrested at once and the wallet is found in his pocket, that constitutes direct evidence. Outside criminal cases the same kind of assured testimony can be cited as direct evidence.

Circumstantial Evidence. In most cases in court such direct evidence is the exception rather than the rule, for a man attempting crime would shun circumstances in which his crime would be witnessed. Indirect evidence—

circumstantial evidence—is much more usual. It lacks the certainty of direct evidence, yet from the known facts presented it is often possible to secure almost the same certainty as from direct evidence. In serious crimes, such as murder, juries are extremely cautious about convicting upon circumstantial evidence. There are many chances of error in making chains of evidence. In indirect evidence a group of facts is presented from which a conclusion is attempted. Suppose a boy had trouble with a farmer and had been heard to threaten to get even. One day the man struck him with a whip as he passed on the road. That night the farmer's barn was set on fire. Neighbors declared they saw some one running from the scene. Next day the boy told his companions he was glad of the loss. Circumstantial evidence points to the boy as the culprit. Yet what might the facts be?

In presenting arguments get as much direct evidence as possible to prove your statements. When direct evidence cannot be secured, link your indirect evidence so closely that it presents not a single weak link. Let the conclusion you draw from it be the only possible one. Make certain no one else can interpret it in any other way.

When you present evidence be sure it completely covers your contention. Be sure it is clear. Be sure it fits in with all the other facts and details presented. Do not let it conflict with usual human experience. Consider the sources of your evidence. If you do not, you can be certain your audience will. Are your sources reliable? Is the information authoritative? Is it first-hand material, or merely hearsay? Is it unprejudiced? Many of the other facts for evidence have already been suggested in the chapter on getting material.

Two General Methods of Reasoning. Frequently the evidence to be used in argumentation must be interpreted before it can be of any value, especially when dealing with propositions of expediency or policy. There are two general methods of reasoning. One is the inductive method, the other the deductive.

Inductive Reasoning. When we discover that a certain operation repeated many times always produces the same result we feel justified in concluding that we can announce it as a universal law. After thousands of falling bodies have been measured and always give the same figures, scientists feel that they may state the law that all falling bodies acquire an acceleration of 32.2 feet per second. This illustrates the inductive method of reasoning. In this system we reason from the specific instance to the general law, from the particular experiment to the universal theory, from the concrete instance to the wide principle.

All modern science is based upon this method—the experimental one. All general theories of any kind today must—to be accepted—be supported by long and careful consideration of all possible and probable circumstances. The theory of evolution as applied to the living things upon the earth is the result of countless observations and experiments.

Hasty Generalization. The speaker cannot himself examine all the specific instances, he cannot consider all the illustrations which might support his position, but he must be careful of a too hasty generalization. Having talked with a dozen returned soldiers he may not declare that all American army men are glad to be out of France, for had he investigated a little further he might have found an equal number who regret the return to this land. He must base his general statement on so many instances that his conclusion will convince not only him, but people disposed to oppose his view. He must be better prepared to show the truth of his declaration than merely to dismiss an example which does not fit into his scheme by glibly asserting that "exceptions prove the rule." He must show that what seems to contradict him is in nature an exception and therefore has nothing at all to do with his rule. Beginning speakers are quite prone to this fault of too hasty generalization.

EXERCISES

1. Write down five general theories or statements which have been established by inductive reasoning.

2. Is there any certainty that they will stand unchanged forever?

3. Under what circumstances are such changes made?

4. Can you cite any accepted laws or theories of past periods which have been overturned?

Deductive Reasoning. After general laws have been established, either by human experience or accepted inductive reasoning, they may be cited as applying to any particular case under consideration. This passing from the general law to the particular instance is deductive reasoning. Deductive reasoning has a regular form called the syllogism.

> Major premise.   All men are mortal.
> Minor premise.   Socrates is a man.
> Conclusion.   Therefore, Socrates is mortal.

If the three parts of a syllogism are correct it has absolute convincing power. Most attempts to disprove its statement attack the first two statements. Although it carries such an air of certainty it is likely to many errors in use. An error like this is common:

> All horses are animals.
> All cows are animals.
> Therefore, all cows are horses.

Explain the fallacy in this syllogism.

Quite as frequently the incorrect syllogism is of this kind.

> The edge of a stream is a bank.
> A bank is a financial institution.
> Therefore, the edge of a stream is a financial institution.

You will comment upon this that its evident silliness would prevent any speaker from using such a form in serious argument. But recall that in the discussion of any idea a term may get its meaning slightly changed. In that slight change of meaning lurks the error illustrated here, ready to lead to false reasoning and weakening of the argument. Certain words of common use are likely to such shifting meanings—*republic, equality, representative, monarchy, socialistic.* Any doubtful passage in which such an error is suspected should be reduced to its syllogistic form to be tested for accuracy.

> A representative of the people must vote always as they would vote.
> A Congressman is a representative of the people.
> Therefore, Congressmen must vote always as the people who elect them would vote.

Is not the expression, *representative of the people,* here used in two different senses?

When an argument is delivered, one of the premises—being a statement which the speaker assumes everyone will admit as true—is sometimes omitted. This shortened form is called an enthymeme.

Smith will be a successful civil engineer for he is a superior mathematician.

Supply the missing premise. Which is it?

In the bald, simple forms here set down, the syllogism and enthymeme are hardly suited to delivery in speeches. They must be amplified, explained, emphasized, in order to serve a real purpose. The following represent better the way a speaker uses deductive reasoning.

> The appointing power is vested in the President and Senate; this is the general rule of the Constitution. The removing power is part of the appointing power; it cannot be separated from the rest.

> DANIEL WEBSTER: *The Appointing and Removing Power*, 1835

Then Daniel Webster stated in rather extended form the conclusion that the Senate should share in the removing proceedings.

> Sir, those who espouse the doctrines of nullification reject, as it seems to me, the first great principle of all republican liberty; that is, that the majority *must* govern. In matters of common concern, the judgment of a majority *must* stand as the judgment of the whole.

> DANIEL WEBSTER: *Reply to Calhoun*, 1853

Then, he argues, as these revenue laws were passed by a majority, they must be obeyed in South Carolina.

Methods of Proof. In extended arguments, just as in detailed exposition, many different methods of proof may be employed.

Explanation. Often a mere clear explanation will induce a listener to accept your view of the truth of a proposition. You have heard men say, "Oh, if that is what you mean, I agree with you entirely. I simply didn't understand you." When you are about to engage in argument consider this method of exposition to see if it will suffice. In all argument there is a great deal of formal or incidental explanation.

Authority. When authority is cited to prove a statement it must be subjected to the same tests in argument as in explanation. Is the authority reliable? Is he unprejudiced? Does his testimony fit in with the circumstances under consideration? Will his statements convince a person likely to be on the opposing side? Why has so much so-called authoritative information concerning conditions in Europe been so discounted? Is it not because the reporters are likely to be prejudiced and because while what they say may be true of certain places and conditions it does not apply to all the points under discussion? The speaker who wants the support of authority will test it as carefully as though its influence is to be used against him—as indeed, it frequently is.

Examples. Where examples are used in argumentation they must serve as more than mere illustrations. In exposition an illustration frequently explains, but that same example would have no value in argument because while it illustrates it does not prove. A suppositious example may serve in explanation; only a fact will serve as proof. The more inevitable its application, the more clinching its effect, the better its argumentative value. Notice how the two examples given below prove that the heirs of a literary man might be the very worst persons to own the copyrights of his writings since as owners they might suppress books which the world of readers should be able to secure easily. While these examples illustrate, do they not also prove?

> I remember Richardson's grandson well; he was a clergyman in the city of London; he was a most upright and excellent man; but he had conceived a strong prejudice against works of fiction. He thought all novel-reading not only frivolous but sinful. He said—this I state on the authority of one of his clerical brethren who is now a bishop—he said that he had never thought it right to read one of his grandfather's books.

> I will give another instance. One of the most instructive, interesting, and delightful books in our language is Boswell's *Life of Johnson*. Now it is well known that Boswell's eldest son considered this book, considered the whole relation of Boswell to Johnson, as a blot in the escutcheon of the family.

Analogy. In argument by analogy the speaker attempts to prove that because certain things are known to be true in something that can be observed they are likely to be true in something else which in so far as it can be observed is quite like the first. We continually argue by analogy in daily life. Lincoln was really using analogy when he replied to the urging to change his army leaders during the Civil War, that he didn't think it wise to "swap horses while crossing a stream." Scientists use this method to draw conclusions when it is impossible to secure from actual observation or experiment a certain last step in the reasoning. The planet Mars and the earth are similar in practically all observable matters; they are about the same distance from the sun, they have the same surface conditions. The earth has living creatures upon it. Hence—so goes the reasoning of analogy—Mars is probably inhabited. Reasoning by analogy is used to prove that universal suffrage is good for the United States because it has been good for one particular state. A student may argue by analogy that the elective system should be introduced into all high schools, because it has been followed in colleges. It may be asserted that a leading bank president will make a good university president, because he has managed one complex institution. The essence of all good reasoning by analogy is that the two things considered must be so nearly alike in all that is known that the presumption of belief is that they must also be alike in the one point the arguer is trying to establish. This is the test he must apply to his own analogy arguments.

> Our community frowns with indignation upon the profaneness of the duel, having its rise in this irrational point of honor. Are you aware that you indulge the same sentiment on a gigantic scale, when you recognize this very point of honor as a proper apology for war? We have already seen that justice is in no respect promoted by war. Is true honor promoted where justice is not?

CHARLES SUMNER: *The True Grandeur of Nations*, 1845

Residues. The method of residues is frequently employed when the speaker is supporting a policy to be carried out, a measure to be adopted, a change to be instituted, or a law to be passed. Granting the assumption that something must be done he considers all the various methods which may be employed, disposes of them one by one as illegal, or unsuited, or clumsy, or inexpedient, leaving only one, the one he wants adopted, as the one which must be followed.

This is a good practical method of proof, provided the speaker really considers *all* the possible ways of proceeding and does show the undesirability of all except the one remaining.

A speaker pleading for the installation of a commission form of city control might list all the possible ways of city government, a business manager, a mayor, a commission. By disposing completely of the first two, he would have proven the need for the last. A good speaker will aways go farther than merely to reach this kind of conclusion. He will, in addition to disproving the unworthy choices, strongly support his residue, the measure he wants adopted. In supporting amounts of taxes, assessments, etc., this method may be used. One amount can be proven so large as to cause unrest, another so small as to be insufficient, a third to produce a total just large enough to meet all anticipated expenses with no surplus for emergencies; therefore the correct amount must be just larger than this but not reaching an amount likely to produce the result caused by the first considered. Used in trials of criminal cases it eliminates motives until a single inevitable remainder cannot be argued away. This may be the clue to follow, or it may be the last one of all suspected persons. Burke considered several possible ways of dealing with the American colonies; one he dismissed as no more than a "sally of anger," a second could not be operated because of the distance, a scheme of Lord North's he proved would complicate rather than settle matters, to change the spirit of America was impossible, to prosecute it as criminal was inexpedient, therefore but one way remained, to conciliate the spirit of discontent by letting the colonies vote their own taxes. It is interesting that what Burke described as the sally of anger was the way the matter was actually settled—Great Britain had to give up the American colonies.

This method is also called elimination.

Cause to Effect. Just as the explainer may pass from cause to effect so may the arguer. Other names for this method are antecedent probability and *a priori* argument. In argument from a known cause an effect is proven as having occurred or as likely to occur. In solving crime this is the method which uses the value of the motives for crime as known to exist in the feelings or sentiments of a certain accused person. A person trying to secure the passage of a certain law will prove that it as the cause will produce certain effects which make it desirable. Changed conditions in the United States will be brought forward as the cause to prove that the Federal government must do things never contemplated by the framers of the Constitution. Great military organization as the cause of the recent war is used now in argument to carry on the plea for the securing of peace by disarmament.

The main difficulty in reasoning from cause to effect is to make the relationship so clear and so close that one thing will be accepted by everybody as the undisputed cause of the alleged effect.

Effect to Cause. In reasoning from effect to cause the reverse method is employed. This is also termed argument from sign or the *a posteriori* method. In it, from some known effect the reasoning proves that it is the result of a certain specified cause. Statistics indicating business prosperity might be used as the effect from which the arguer proves that they are caused by a high protective tariff. A speaker shows the good effects upon people to prove that certain laws—claimed as the causes—should be extended in application. Arguments from effect to cause may be extremely far reaching; as every effect leads to some cause, which is itself the effect of some other cause, and so on almost to infinity. The good speaker will use just those basic causes which prove his proposition—no more.

In actual practice the two forms of reasoning from cause to effect and from effect to cause are frequently combined to make the arguments all the more convincing. Grouped together they are termed causal relations.

Persuasion. When a speaker has conclusively proven what he has stated in his proposition, is his speech ended? In some cases, yes; in many cases, no. Mere proof appeals to the intellect only; it settles matters perhaps, but leaves the hearer cold and humanly inactive. He may feel like saying,

"Well, even if what you say is true, what are you going to do about it?" Mathematical and scientific proofs exist for mere information, but most arguments delivered before audiences have a purpose. They try to make people do something. A group of people should be aroused to some determination of purposeful thought if not to a registered act at the time. In days of great stress the appeal to action brought the immediate response in military enlistments; in enrollment for war work; in pledges of service; in signing membership blanks and subscription blanks; in spontaneous giving.

Persuasion Produces a Response. The end of most argumentative speaking is to produce a response. It may be the casting of a vote, the joining of a society, the repudiation of an unworthy candidate, the demonstrating of the solidarity of labor, the affiliating with a religious sect, the changing of a mode of procedure, the purchasing of a new church organ, the wearing of simpler fashions, or any of the thousand and one things a patient listener is urged to do in the course of his usual life.

When the speaker passes on from mere convincing to appealing for some response he has passed from argumentation to persuasion. Nearly every argumentative speech dealing with a proposition of policy shows first what ought to be done, then tries to induce people to do it, by appealing as strongly as possible to their practical, esthetic, or moral interests. All such interests depend upon what we call sentiments or feelings to which worthy —note the word *worthy*—appeals may legitimately be addressed. Attempts to arouse unworthy motives by stirring up ignorance and prejudice are always to be most harshly condemned. Such practices have brought certain kinds of so-called persuasion into well-deserved contempt. The high sounding spell-binder with his disgusting spread-eagleism cannot be muzzled by law, but he may be rendered harmless by vacant chairs and empty halls. Real eloquence is not a thing of noise and exaggeration. Beginning speakers should avoid the tawdry imitation as they would a plague.

Elements of Persuasion. What elements may aid the persuasive power of a speech? First of all, the occasion may be just the right one. The surroundings may have prepared the audience for the effect the speaker should make if he knows how to seize upon the opportunity for his own purpose. The speaker must know how to adapt himself to the circumstances present. In other cases, he must be able to do the much more difficult thing—adapt the circumstances to his purpose.

Secondly, the subject matter itself may prepare for the persuasive treatment in parts. Everyone realizes this. When emotional impulses are present in the material the introduction of persuasion is inevitable and fitting, if not overdone.

Thirdly, the essence of persuasion depends upon the speaker. All the good characteristics of good speaking will contribute to the effect of his attempts at persuasion. A good speaker is sincere to the point of winning respect even when he does not carry conviction. He is in earnest. He is simple and unaffected. He has tact. He is fair to every antagonistic attitude. He has perfect self-control. He does not lose his temper. He can show a proper sense of humor. He has genuine sympathy. And finally—perhaps it includes all the preceding—he has personal magnetism.

With such qualities a speaker can make an effective appeal by means of persuasion. If upon self-criticism and self-examination, or from outside kindly comment, he concludes he is lacking in any one of these qualities he should try to develop it.

EXERCISES

Prepare and deliver speeches upon some of the following or upon propositions suggested by them. If the speech is short, try to employ only one method of proof, but make it convincing. Where suitable, add persuasive elements.

1. Make a proposition from one of the following topics. Deliver an argumentative speech upon it. The next election. Entrance to college. Child labor. The study of the classics. The study of science.

2. Recommend changes which will benefit your school, your club or society, your church, your town, your state.

3. The Japanese should be admitted to the United States upon the same conditions as other foreigners.

4. Men and women should receive the same pay for the same work done.

5. All church property should be taxed.

6. All laws prohibiting secular employment on Sunday should be repealed.

7. The purely protective tariff should be withdrawn from goods the manufacture of which has been firmly established in this country.

8. Large incomes should be subject to a graduated income tax.

9. Employers should not be forced to recognize labor unions.

10. Immigration into the United States of persons who cannot read or write some language should be prohibited, except dependents upon such qualified entrants.

11. An amendment should be added to the Constitution providing for uniform marriage and divorce laws throughout the entire country.

12. A city is the best place for a college.

13. Military training should be obligatory in all public schools.

14. Colleges and universities should reduce the attention paid to athletics.

15. The negro in the South should be disfranchised.

16. The number of Representatives in Congress should be reduced.

17. Moving pictures should be used in schools.

18. Street car systems should be owned and operated by municipalities.

19. Education should be compulsory until the completion of high school.

20. Athletes whose grade is below 75% should be debarred from all participation until the marks are raised.

21. The Federal government should own and operate the telegraph and telephone systems.

22. The state should provide pensions for indigent mothers of children below the working age.

23. The study of algebra (or some other subject) in the high school should be elective.

24 The initiative should be adopted in all states.

25. The referendum should be adopted in all states.

26. All governmental officials should be subject to recall.

27. The public should support in all ways the movement of labor to secure the closed shop system.

28. Railroad crossings should be abolished.

29. The Federal government should pass laws controlling all prices of foodstuffs.

30. A trial before a group of competent judges should be substituted for trial by jury.

CHAPTER XI

REFUTING

Answering the Other Side. It has been said already that even in a single argumentative speech some account must be taken of the possibility among the audience of the belief in other views. A speaker must always assume that people will believe otherwise than he does. In such cases as debate or questioning after a speech is made, this opposing side will very clearly be brought out, so that any person training for any kind of public speaking will give much attention to the contentions of others in order to strengthen his own convictions as displayed in his speeches.

A sincere thinker may believe that trial before a group of competent judges is a better procedure than trial by jury. Were he to speak upon such a proposition he would realize that he would meet at once the solid opposition of the general opinion that jury trials, sanctioned by long practice, are in some mysterious way symbolic of the liberty and equality of mankind. Before he could expect to arouse sympathetic understanding he would have to answer all the possible objections and reasons against his new scheme. This he would do by refutation, by disproving the soundness of the arguments against his scheme. He could cite the evident and recorded injustices committed by juries. He could bring before them the impossibility of securing an intelligent verdict from a group of farmers, anxious to get to their farms for harvest, sitting in a case through July, while the days passed in lengthy examinations of witnesses—one man was on the stand eight days —and the lawyers bandied words and names like socialist, pagan, bolsheviki, anarchy, ideal republic, Aristotle, Plato, Herbert Spencer, Karl Marx, Tolstoi, Jane Addams, Lenin. Then when he felt assured he had removed all the reasons for supporting the present jury system he could proceed to advance his own substitute.

Need and Value of Refutation. In all argumentation, therefore, refutation is valuable and necessary. By it opposing arguments are reasoned away, their real value is determined, or they are answered and demolished if they are false or faulty. To acquire any readiness as a speaker or debater a person must pay a great deal of attention to refutation. It has also an additional value. It has been stated that every argumentative speaker must study the other side of every question upon which he is to speak. One great debater declared that if he had time to study only one side of a proposition or law case he would devote that time to the other side. Study your own position from the point of view of the other side. Consider carefully what arguments that side will naturally advance. In fact, try to refute your own arguments exactly as some opponent would, or get some friend to try to refute your statements. Many a speaker has gained power in reasoning by having his views attacked by members of his family who would individually and collectively try to drive him into a corner. In actual amount, perhaps you will never deliver as much refutation of an opponent as you will conjure up in your mind against your own speeches. Perhaps, also, this great amount advanced by you in testing your own position will prevent your opponents from ever finding in your delivered arguments much against which they can pit their own powers of refutation.

In judging your own production you will have to imagine yourself on the other side, so the methods will be the same for all purposes of self-help or weakening of an opponent's views.

Contradiction Is Not Refutation. In the first place contradiction is not refutation. No unsupported fact or statement has any value in argumentation. Such expressions as "I don't believe, I don't think so, I don't agree" introduce not arguments, but personal opinions. You must, to make your refutation valuable, *prove* your position. Never allow your attempts at refutation to descend to mere denial or quibbling. Be prepared to support, to prove everything you say.

Three Phases of Refutation. In general, refutation consists of three phases:

1. The analysis of the opposite side.
2. The classification of the arguments according to importance.
3. The answering of only the strongest points.

Analysis of Opposing Side for Accuracy. In the first analysis, you will probably examine the opposing statements to test their accuracy. Mere slips, so evident that they deceive no one, you may disregard entirely, but gross error of fact or conclusion you should note and correct in unmistakably plain terms. The kind of statement which gives insufficient data should be classed in analysis with this same kind of erroneous statement. A shoe dealer in arguing for increased prices might quote correctly the rising cost of materials, but if he stopped there, you in refutation should be able to show that profits had already risen to 57%, and so turn his own figures against him. Another class of refutation similar to this is the questioning of authorities. Something concerning this has already been said. In a recent trial a lawyer cast doubt upon the value of a passage read from a book by declaring its author could never have written such a thing. In refutation the opposing lawyer said, "You will find that passage on page 253 of his *Essays and Letters.*" Public speakers, realizing that errors of statement are likely to be the first to be picked out for correction, and recognizing the damaging effect of such conviction in error of fact and testimony, are extremely careful not to render themselves liable to attack upon such points. Yet they may. We are told by Webster's biographers that in later periods of his life he was detected in errors of law in cases being argued before the court, and refuted in statement. To catch such slips requires two things of the successful speaker. He must be in possession of the facts himself. He must be mentally alert to see the falsity and know how to answer it.

Begging the Question. The expression "begging the question" is often heard as a fallacy in argument. In its simplest form it is similar to inaccurate statement, for it includes assertions introduced without proof, and the statement of things as taken for granted without attempting to prove them, yet using them to prove other statements. Sometimes, also, a careless thinker, through an extended group of paragraphs will end by taking as proven exactly the proposition he started out to prove, when close analysis will show that nowhere during the discussion does he actually prove it. As this is frequent in amateur debates, students should be on their guard against it.

Ignoring the Question. The same kind of flimsy mental process results in ignoring the question. Instead of sticking closely to the proposition to be proved the speaker argues beside the point, proving not the entire proposition but merely a portion of it. Or in some manner he may shift his ground and emerge, having proven the wrong point or something he did not start out to consider. An amateur theatrical producer whose playhouse had been closed by the police for violating the terms of his license started out to defend his action, but ended by proving that all men are equal. In fact he wound up by quoting the poem by Burns, "A Man's a Man for A' That." Such a shifting of propositions is a frequent error of speakers. It occurs so often that one might be disposed to term it a mere trick to deceive, or a clever though unscrupulous device to secure support for a weak claim. One of the first ways for the speaker to avoid it is to be able to recognize it when it occurs. One of the most quoted instances of its effective unmasking is the following by Macaulay.

> The advocates of Charles, like the advocates of other malefactors against whom overwhelming evidence is produced, generally decline all controversy about the facts, and content themselves with calling testimony to character. He had so many private virtues! And had James the Second no private virtues! Was Oliver Cromwell, his bitterest enemies themselves being judges, destitute of private virtues? And what, after all, are the virtues ascribed to Charles? A religious zeal, not more sincere than that of his son, and fully as weak and narrow-minded, and a few of the ordinary household decencies which half the tombstones in England claim for those who lie beneath them. A good father! A good husband! Ample apologies indeed for fifteen years of persecution, tyranny, and falsehood!

> We charge him with having broken his coronation oath; and we are told that he kept his marriage vow! We accuse him of having given up his people to merciless inflictions of the most hot-headed and hard-hearted of prelates; and the defence is, that he took his little son on his knee and kissed him! We censure him for having violated the articles of the Petition of Right, after having, for good and valuable consideration, promised to observe them; and we are informed that he was accustomed to hear prayers at six o'clock in the morning! It is to such considerations as these, together with his Vandyke dress, his handsome face, and his peaked beard, that he owes, we verily believe, most of his popularity with the present generation.

Appealing to Prejudice or Passions. The question is also ignored when the speaker appeals to the prejudices or passions of his audience (*argumentum ad populum*). Persons of some intellect resent this as almost an insult if they are in the audience, yet it is often resorted to by speakers who would rather produce the effect they desire by the use of any methods, right or wrong. Its use in court by unscrupulous lawyers to win decisions is checked by attempts on the part of judges to counteract it in their charges to the jury, but its influence may still persist. Mark Antony in Shakespere's play, *Julius Caesar*, used it in his oration over the dead body of Caesar to further his own ends.

Taking Advantage of Ignorance. Just as a speaker may take advantage of the prejudices and passions of an audience, so he may take advantage of their ignorance. Against the blankness of their brains he may hurl unfamiliar names to dazzle them, cite facts of all kinds to impress them, show a wide knowledge of all sorts of things, "play up to them" in every way, until they become so impressed that they are ready to accept as truth anything he chooses to tell them. Any daily paper will provide examples of the sad results of the power of this kind of fallacious reasoning. The get-rich-quick schemes, the worthless stock deals, the patent medicine quacks, the extravagantly worded claims of new religions and faddist movements, all testify to the power this form of seemingly convincing argument has over the great mass of the ignorant.

The Fallacy of Tradition. In discussing the burden of proof it was said that such burden rests upon the advocate of change, or novel introductions, etc. This tendency of the people at large to be rather conservative in practice links with the fallacy of tradition, the belief that whatever is, is right. In many cases such a faith is worse than wrong, it is pernicious. Many of the questions concerning relations of modern society—as capital and labor—are based upon this fallacy. Henry Clay was guilty of it when he announced, "Two hundred years of legislation have sanctioned and sanctified negro slaves as property." The successful way to dispose of such a fallacy is illustrated by William Ellery Channing's treatment of this statement.

> But this property, we are told, is not to be questioned on account
> of its long duration. "Two hundred years of legislation have
> sanctioned and sanctified negro slaves as property." Nothing but

respect for the speaker could repress criticism on this unhappy phraseology. We will trust it escaped him without thought. But to confine ourselves to the argument from duration; how obvious the reply! Is injustice changed into justice by the practice of the ages? Is my victim made a righteous prey because I have bowed him to the earth till he cannot rise? For more than two hundred years heretics were burned, and not by mobs, not by lynch law, but by the decrees of the councils, at the instigation of theologians, and with the sanction of the laws and religions of nations; and was this a reason for keeping up the fires, that they had burned two hundred years? In the Eastern world successive despots, not for two hundred years, but for twice two thousand have claimed the right of life and death over millions, and, with no law but their own will, have beheaded, bowstrung, starved, tortured unhappy men without number who have incurred their wrath; and does the lapse of so many centuries sanctify murder and ferocious power?

Attacking a Speaker's Character or Principles. Sometimes a speaker who finds himself unable to attack the truth of a proposition, or the arguments cited to support it, changes his tactics from the subject-matter to the opponent himself and delivers an attack upon his character, principles, or former beliefs and statements. This is called the *argumentum ad hominem*. In no sense is it really argument; it is irrelevant attack, and should be answered in a clear accurate demonstration of its unsuitability to the topic under consideration. It is unworthy, of course, but it is a tempting device for the speaker who can combine with it an appeal to the prejudices or passions of his audience.

The author has seen the entire population of Rome agitated because in a Senatorial debate one speaker attacked the family reputation of one of his opponents—a matter which, even if true, certainly had nothing to do with the bill under discussion. Political campaigns used to be disgraced by a prevalence of such appeals for votes. We may pride ourselves upon an advance in such matters, but there is still too much of it to let us congratulate ourselves upon our political good manners. You cannot ascribe bad faith to a man who argues now from a different attitude from the one he formerly supported. Changes of conviction are frequent in all matters. A man must be judged by the reasons he gives for his position at any one time. Many a person, who ten years ago would have argued against it, now believes a League of Nations possible and necessary. Many a person who a few years back could see no advantage in labor organizations is anxious now to join an affiliated union.

If you find the suggestion of such an attack in any of your own speeches, cast it out. If it is ever used against you, refute it by the strength of arguments you deliver in support of your position. Remove all assertions which do not relate to the debated topic. Make your audience sympathize with your repudiation of the remarks of your opponent, even though he has succeeded in delivering them.

Fallacies of Causal Relationship. The various fallacies that may be committed under the relation of cause and effect are many. Just because something happened prior to something else (the effect), the first may be mistakenly quoted as the cause. Or the reverse may be the error—the second may be assumed to be the effect of the first. The way to avoid this fallacy was suggested in the discussion of explanation by means of cause and effect where the statement was made that two events must not be merely *sequential*, they must be *consequential*. In argument the slightest gap in the apparent relationship is likely to result in poor reasoning, and the consequent fallacy may be embodied in the speech. When people argue to prove that superstitions have come true, do they present clear reasoning to show conclusively that the alleged cause—such as sitting thirteen at table— actually produced the effect of a death? Do they *establish* a close causal relationship, or do they merely *assert* that after a group of thirteen had sat at table some one did die? Mathematically, would the law of chance or probability not indicate that such a thing would happen a little less surely if the number had been twelve, a little more surely if fourteen?

Common sense, clear headedness, logical reasoning, and a wide knowledge of all kinds of things will enable a speaker to recognize these fallacies, anticipate them, and successfully refute them.

Methods of Refuting. Having found the fallacies in an argument you should proceed to refute them. Just how you can best accomplish your purpose of weakening your opponent's position, of disposing of his arguments, of answering his contentions, must depend always upon the particular circumstances of the occasion, of the material presented, of the attitude of the judges or audience, of your opponent himself, and of the purpose you are striving to accomplish. Practice, knowledge, skill, will in such cases all serve your end. You should be able to choose, and effectively use the best. It is impossible to anticipate and provide for all the possibilities, but a few of the most common probabilities and the methods of dealing with them can be here set down.

Courteous Correction. In case of apparent error or over-sight you will do well to be courteous rather than over-bearing and dictatorial in your correction. Never risk losing an advantage by driving your audience into sympathy for your opponent by any manner of your own. A newspaper discussing the objections made to the covenant of the League of Nations points out an over-sight in this way: "How did Senator Knox happen to overlook the fact that his plan for compulsory arbitration is embodied in Article XII of the proposed covenant?"

Refuting Incorrect Analogy. The caution was given that reasoning from analogy must show the complete correspondence in all points possible of the known from which the reasoning proceeds to the conclusion about the unknown, which then is to be accepted as true. Unless that complete correspondence is established firmly the speaker is likely to have his carefully worked out analogy demolished before his eyes. Notice how such refutation is clearly demonstrated in the following.

> So it does; but the sophistry here is plain enough, although it is not always detected. Great genius and force of character undoubtedly make their own career. But because Walter Scott was dull at school, is a parent to see with joy that his son is a dunce? Because Lord Chatham was of a towering conceit, must we infer that pompous vanity portends a comprehensive statesmanship that will fill the world with the splendor of its triumphs? Because Sir Robert Walpole gambled and swore and boozed at Houghton, are we to suppose that gross sensuality and coarse contempt of human nature are the essential secrets of a power that defended liberty against tory intrigue and priestly politics? Was it because Benjamin Franklin was not college-bred

that he drew the lightning from heaven and tore the scepter from the tyrant? Was it because Abraham Lincoln had little schooling that his great heart beat true to God and man, lifting him to free a race and die for his country? Because men naturally great have done great service in the world without advantages, does it follow that lack of advantage is the secret of success?

GEORGE WILLIAM CURTIS: The Public Duty of Educated Men, 1877

Reducing Proof to Absurdity. A very good way of showing the unreliability of an opposing argument is to pretend to accept it as valid, then carrying it on to a logical conclusion, to show that its end proves entirely too much, or that it reduces the entire chain of reasoning to absurdity. This is, in fact, called *reductio ad absurdum*. At times the conclusion is so plainly going to be absurd that the refuter need not carry its successive steps into actual delivery. In speaking to large groups of people nothing is better than this for use as an effective weapon. It gives the hearers the feeling that they have assisted in the damaging demonstration. It almost seems as though the speaker who uses it were merely using—as he really is— material kindly presented to him by his opponent. So the two actually contribute in refuting the first speaker's position.

> Congress only can declare war; therefore, when one State is at war with a foreign nation, all must be at war. The President and the Senate only can make peace; when peace is made for one State, therefore, it must be made for all.

> Can anything be conceived more preposterous, than that any State should have power to nullify the proceedings of the general government respecting peace and war? When war is declared by a law of Congress, can a single State nullify that law, and remain at peace? And yet she may nullify that law as well as any other. If the President and Senate make peace, may one State, nevertheless, continue the war? And yet, if she can nullify a law, she may quite as well nullify a treaty.

DANIEL WEBSTER: The Constitution Not a Compact between Sovereign States, 1833

Lincoln could always use this method of *reductio ad absurdum* most effectively because he seldom failed to accentuate the absurdity by some instance which made clear to the least learned the force of his argument. Many of his best remembered quaint and picturesque phrases were embodied in his serious demolition of some high-handed presumption of a political leader.

> Under all these circumstances, do you really feel yourselves justified to break up this government unless such a court decision as yours is shall be at once submitted to as a conclusive and final rule of political action? But you will not abide the election of a Republican President! In that supposed event, you say, you will destroy the Union; and then, you say, the great crime of having destroyed it will be upon us! That is cool. A highwayman holds a pistol to my ear, and mutters through his teeth, "Stand and deliver, or I shall kill you, and then you will be a murderer!"

ABRAHAM LINCOLN: *Cooper Union Speech*, 1860

Amplifying and Diminishing. Finally a good method of refuting the claim of importance made for an opposing proposition is by amplifying and diminishing. In plain terms this depends upon contrast in which you reduce the value of the opposing idea and emphasize the value of your own. An excellent use for this is as a rapid summary at the end of your speech, where it will leave in the hearer's mind an impression of the comparative value of the two views he has heard discussed, with an inevitable sense of the unquestioned worth of one above the other. Burke sums up his extended refutations of Lord North's plan for dealing with America in these telling contrasts.

> Compare the two. This I offer to give you is plain and simple; the other full of perplexed and intricate mazes. This is mild; that harsh. This found by experience effectual for its purposes; the other is a new project. This is universal; the other calculated for certain colonies only. This is immediate in its conciliatory operation; the other remote, contingent, full of hazard. Mine is

what becomes the dignity of a ruling people—gratuitous, unconditional—and not held out as a matter of bargain and sale.

EDMUND BURKE: Conciliation with America, 1775

Position of Refutation in the Speech. The position of refutation in the finished speech will depend always upon the nature of the proposition, the exact method of the refutation, and the audience. If you are making the only speech upon the proposition and you feel that the audience may have a slight prejudice against what you are about to urge, you may gain adherents at once by refuting at the beginning the possible arguments in their minds. By this procedure you will clear the field for your own operations. To change the figure of speech, you erase from the slate what is already written there, so that you may place upon it your own speech and its convictions.

If you are debating and the speaker just before you has evidently made the judges accept his arguments, again you might remove that conviction by refutation before you proceed to build up your own side. If your regular arguments meet his squarely, proceed as you had planned, but be sure when any reasoning you offer nullifies any he has delivered, that you call the attention of the audience to the fact that you have wiped out his score. In this way your constructive argument and refutation will proceed together. You will save valuable time.

Constructive Argument Is More Valuable than Refutation. Often the rebuttal speeches of debate, coming at the close of the regular debate speeches, seem reserved for all the refutation. This is certainly the place for much refutation, certainly not all. The last speakers of the rebuttal speeches should never rest content with leaving only refutation in the hearers' minds. If they do, the debate may leave the condition entirely where it was at the beginning, for theoretically every argument advanced by either side has been demolished by the other. After the rebuttal the last points left with the judges should be constructive arguments.

In a single speech the refutation may be delivered in sections as the demands of coherence and the opportunities for emphasis may suggest. Here again, always make the last section a constructive one with arguments in support of your proposition.

CHAPTER XII

DEBATING

The Ideal of Debating. A long time ago so admirable a man as William Penn stated the high ideal of all real debating whether practised in the limited range of school interests or in the extended field of life's activities.

> In all debates let truth be thy aim, not victory, or an unjust interest; and endeavor to gain, rather than to expose thy antagonist.

The quotation states exactly the true aim of all debating—the conclusion of the right, the truth rather than the securing of a decision over an opponent. The same rules which animate the true lover of sports, the clear distinction which is instilled into all participants of amateur athletics of the meanings and significance of the two terms *sportsman* and *sport*, can be carried over to apply to school activities in debating. Honest differences of opinion among people upon countless questions will always furnish enough material for regular debating so that no one need ever do violence to his convictions.

Value of Debate. One of the greatest educational values of practice in debate is that the ability it develops can be applied instantly in the life beyond the schoolroom, that it operates in every person's daily life. There are differences in the manner in which debating is carried on in the two places, but practice in the earlier will result in skill and self-confidence in the second.

Debate in Actual Life. The most marked difference between debates in the two phases of life is the difference of form. In academic circles debate is a well-regulated game between matched sides. In actual life only in certain professions are the rules well defined. In most cases the debating is disguised under different forms, though the essential purposes and methods are the same.

Debate between lawyers in courts—technically termed pleading—is the most formal of all professional debating. Its regulations are found in the stabilized court procedure which every lawyer must master and obey.

Much looser than the formal debate of the court room is the speech-making of the legislative organization from the lowest township board meeting up to the Senate of the United States. Of course the members of such bodies are regulated by certain restrictions, but the speeches are not likely to be curbed in time as are academic performances, nor are the speakers likely to follow a prearranged order, nor are they always equally balanced in number, nor do they agree so carefully upon "team work." Sometimes in a legislative body the first speaker may be on the negative side, which is quite contrary to all the rules of regularly conducted debates. All the speakers may also be on one side of a measure, the opposing side not deigning to reply, resting secure in the knowledge of how many votes they can control when the real test of power comes.

Most informal of all are the general discussions in which business matters are decided. In these the speeches are never so set as in the two preceding kinds. The men are less formal in their relations and addresses to one another. The steps are less marked in their changes. Yet underneath the seeming lack of regulation there is the framework of debate, for there is always present the sense of two sides upon every proposition, whether it be the purchase of new office equipment for a distant agent, an increase of salary for employees, or the increase of capitalization. Certain speakers support some proposition. Others oppose it until they are convinced and won over to the affirmative side, or until they are out-voted.

Two men seated in an office may themselves be debaters, audience, and judges of their own argumentative opinions. They may in themselves fill all the requirements of a real debate. They deliver the speeches on the affirmative and negative sides. Each listens to the arguments of his opponent. And finally, the pair together give a decision upon the merits of the arguments presented.

On all such occasions the speakers need and use just those qualities which classroom training has developed in them—knowledge of material, plan of presentation, skill in expression, conviction and persuasion of manner, graceful acceptance of defeat.

Debating Demands a Decision. Debating goes one step farther than merely argumentative speaking. Debating demands a decision upon the case, it requires a judgment, a registered action. Again in this respect it is like a game.

EXERCISES

1. Make a list of propositions which have been debated or might be debated in a courtroom.

2. Make another list of propositions which have been debated or might be debated in legislative bodies.

3. Make a list of propositions which might be debated in business.

4. As far as is possible, indicate the decisions upon them.

5. Choose some proposition on which there is considerable difference of opinion in the class. Make a list of those who favor and those who oppose. Speak upon the proposition, alternating affirmative and negative.

6. Discuss the speeches delivered in the fifth exercise.

Persons Involved in a Debate. Who are the persons involved in a regular debate? They are the presiding officer, the speakers themselves, the audience, the judges.

The Presiding Officer. Every debate has a presiding officer. The Vice-President of the United States is the presiding officer of the Senate. The Speaker is the presiding officer of the House of Representatives. If you will refer to Chapter IV on *Beginning the Speech* you will see several other titles of presiding officers. In school debates the head of the institution may act in that capacity, or some person of note may be invited to preside. In regular classroom work the instructor may serve as presiding officer, or some member of the class may be chosen or appointed. The latter method is the best—after the instructor has shown by example just what the duties of such a position are.

The presiding officer should announce the topic of debate in a short introductory speech. He should read the names of the speakers on the affirmative and those on the negative side. He should stipulate the terms of the debate—length of each speech, time for rebuttal, order of rebuttal, method of keeping speakers within time limits, conditions of judgment (material, presentation, etc.), announce the judges, and finally introduce the first speaker; then the subsequent speakers. At the close he might refer to the fact of the debate's being ended, he might rehearse the conditions of judgment, and request the judges to retire to consider their decision. Practice varies as to who shall deliver the decision of the judges to the audience. Sometimes the chairman elected by the judges announces the decision. Sometimes the judges hand the decision to the presiding officer who announces it.

The Debaters. Beyond saying that the speakers must do their best, there is nothing to be added here about their duty in the debate except to issue one warning to them in connection with the next personal element to be considered—the audience.

The Audience. Debaters must remember that in practically no circumstances outside legislative bodies are the audience and the judges ever the same. Debaters argue to convince the judges—not the entire audience, who are really as disconnected from the decision of the debate as are the straggling spectators and listeners in a courtroom detached from the jury who render the verdict of guilty or not guilty. The debater must therefore speak for the judges, not for his audience. Many a debating team has in the course of its speeches won all the applause only to be bitterly disappointed in the end by hearing the decision awarded to the other side. Recall the warnings given in the previous chapters against the tempting fallacies of appealing to crowd feelings and prejudices.

In classroom debates it is a good distribution of responsibility to make all the members not participating in the speaking act as judges and cast votes in rendering a decision. This makes the judges and the audience one. Moreover it changes the mere listener into a discriminating judge. If the instructor cares to carry this matter of responsibility one step farther, he can ask the members of the class to explain and justify their votes.

The audience, when it is also the judge, has the responsibility of careful attention, analysis, and comparison. It is too much to expect usual general audiences to refuse to be moved by unworthy pleas and misrepresentations, to accord approval only to the best speakers and the soundest arguments. But surely in a class of public speakers any such tricks and schemes should be received with stolid frigidity. Nothing is so damaging to appeals to prejudice, spread-eagleism, and fustian bombast as an impassive reception.

The Judges. In any debate the judges are of supreme importance. They decide the merits of the speakers themselves. The judges are of infinitely more importance than the audience. In interscholastic debates men of some prominence are invited to act as judges. In the instructions to them it should be made clear that they are not to decide which side of a proposition they themselves approve. They are to decide which group of speakers does the best work. They should try to be merely the impersonal registers of comparative merit. They should sink their own feelings as every teacher must when he hears a good speech from one of his own students supporting something to which the instructor is opposed. Good judges of debates realize this and frequently award decisions to speakers who support opposite positions to their personal opinions. They must not be like the judges in an interscholastic debate who announced their decision thus, "The judges have decided that China must not be dismembered." That was an interesting fact perhaps, but it had nothing to do with their duty as judges of that debate.

In business, the buyer, the head of the department, the board of directors, constitute the judges who render the decision. In legislative assemblies the audience and judges are practically identical, for after the debate upon a measure is concluded, those who have listened to it render individual verdicts by casting their votes. In such cases we frequently see decisions rendered not upon the merits of the debate, but according to class prejudice, personal opinion, or party lines. This is why so many great argumentative speeches were accounted failures at the time of their delivery. Delivered to secure majority votes they failed to carry conviction to the point of changing immediate action, and so in the small temporary sense they were failures. In legal trials the jury is the real judge, although by our peculiar misapplication of the term a different person entirely is called judge. In court the judge is in reality more often merely the presiding officer. He oversees the observance of all the rules of court practice, keeps lawyers within the regulations, instructs the jury, receives the decision from them, and then applies the law. Every lawyer speaks—not to convince the judge—but to convince the jury to render a decision in his favor.

Scholastic Debating. Choosing the Proposition. In school debating the proposition may be assigned by the instructor or it may be chosen by him from a number submitted by the class. The class itself may choose by vote a proposition for debate. In interscholastic debating the practice now usually followed is for one school to submit the proposition and for the second school to decide which side it prefers to support. In any method the aim should be to give neither side any advantage over the other. The speakers upon the team may be selected before the question of debate is known. It seems better, when possible, to make the subject known first and then secure as speakers upon both sides, students who have actual beliefs upon the topic. Such personal conviction always results in keener rivalry.

Time Limits. Since no debate of this kind must last too long, time restrictions must be agreed upon. In every class, conditions will determine these terms. Three or four speakers upon each side make a good team. If each is allowed six minutes the debate should come well within an hour and still allow some time for voting upon the presentations. It should be distinctly understood that a time limit upon a speaker must be observed by him or be enforced by the presiding officer.

The speakers upon one side will arrange among themselves the order in which they will speak but there should be a clear understanding beforehand as to whether rebuttal speeches are to be allowed.

Rebuttal Speeches. Rebuttal speeches are additional speeches allowed to some or all the speakers of a debating team after the regular argumentative speeches have been delivered. In an extended formal debate all the speakers may thus appear a second time. In less lengthy discussions only some of them may be permitted to appear a second time. As the last speaker has the advantage of making the final impression upon the judges it is usual to offset this by reversing the order of rebuttal. In the first speeches the negative always delivers the last speech. Sometimes the first affirmative speaker is allowed to follow with the single speech in rebuttal. If the team consist of three speakers and all are allowed to appear in rebuttal the entire order is as follows.

First Part	*Rebuttal*
First affirmative	First negative
First negative	First affirmative
Second affirmative	Second negative
Second negative	Second affirmative
Third affirmative	Third negative
Third negative	Third affirmative

If not all the speakers are to speak in rebuttal the team itself decides which of its members shall speak for all.

Preparation. The proposition should be decided on and the teams selected long enough in advance to allow for adequate preparation. Every means should be employed to secure sufficient material in effective arrangement. Once constituted, the team should consider itself a unit. Work should be planned in conference and distributed among the speakers. At frequent meetings they should present to the side all they are able to find. They should lay out a comprehensive plan of support of their own side. They should anticipate the arguments likely to be advanced by the other, and should provide for disposing of them if they are important enough to require refuting. It is a good rule for every member of a debating team to know all the material on his side, even though part of it is definitely assigned to another speaker.

This preliminary planning should be upon a definite method. A good outline to use, although some parts may be discarded in the debate itself, is the following simple one.

    I. State the proposition clearly.
        1. Define the terms.
        2. Explain it as a whole.
   II. Give a history of the case.

1. Show its present bearing or aspect.
III. State the issues.
IV. Prove.
V. Refute.
VI. Conclude.

Finding the Issues. In debating, since time is so valuable, a speaker must not wander afield. He must use all his ability, all his material to prove his contention. It will help him to reject material not relevant if he knows exactly what is at issue between the two sides. It was avoiding the issue to answer the charge that Charles I was a tyrant by replying that he was a good husband. Unless debaters realize exactly what must be proven to make their position secure, there will be really no debate, for the two sides will never meet in a clash of opinion. They will pass each other without meeting, and instead of a debate they will present a series of argumentative speeches. This failure to state issues clearly and to support or refute them convincingly is one of the most common faults of all debating. In ordinary conversation a frequently heard criticism of a discussion or speech or article is "But that was not the point at issue at all." These issues must appear in the preliminary plans, in the finished brief, and in the debate itself.

The only point in issue between us is, how long after an author's death the State shall recognize a copyright in his representatives and assigns; and it can, I think, hardly be disputed by any rational man that this is a point which the legislature is free to determine in the way which may appear to be most conducive to the general good.

THOMAS BABINGTON MACAULAY: Copyright, 1841

Mr. President, the very first question that challenges our attention in the matter of a league of nations is the question of whether a war in Europe is a matter of concern to the United States. The ultraopponents of any league of nations assert that European quarrels and European battles are no concern of ours. If that be true, we may well pause before obligating ourselves to make them our concern. Is it true?

SENATOR P.J. MCCUMBER: The League of Nations, 1919

The best method of finding the issues is to put down in two columns the main contentions of both sides. By eliminating those entries which are least important and those which have least bearing upon the present case the issues may be reduced to those which the debate should cover. Any possible attempt to cloud the issues on the part of the opposing side can thus be forestalled. All the speakers on one side should participate in this analysis of the proposition to find and state the issues.

The New York *Tribune*, by parallel columns, brought out these chief points of difference between the Paris plan and Senator Knox's for the League of Nations.

THE KNOX PLAN	THE PARIS PLAN
League formed of all, not a portion, of the nations of the world.	Under Article VII it is provided that no state shall be admitted unless it is able to give guaranties

War to be declared an international crime, and any nation engaging in war, except in self-defense when actually attacked, to be punished by the world as an international criminal.

The Monroe Doctrine to be safeguarded; also our immigration policy and our right to expel aliens.

of its intention to observe its international obligations and conform to the principles prescribed by the League in regard to it's naval and military forces and armaments.

Article XVI provides that should any of the high contracting parties break covenants under Article XII (relating to arbitration) it shall be deemed to have committed an act of war against the League, which undertakes to exercise economic pressure; and it is to be the duty of the executive council to recommend what military or naval force the members of the League shall contribute to be used to protect the covenants of the League.

None of these matters is mentioned specifically, but President Wilson has said that the League will "extend the Monroe Doctrine to the whole world" and that domestic and internal questions are not a concern of the League.

Our right to maintain military and naval establishments and coaling stations, and our right to fortify the Panama Canal and our frontiers to be safeguarded.

Article VIII says: "The executive council shall also determine for the consideration and action of the several governments what military equipment and armament is fair and reasonable and in proportion to the scale of forces laid down in the program of disarmament, and these limits when adopted shall not be exceeded without the permission of the executive council."

An international court to be empowered by the League to call upon the signatory Powers to enforce its decrees against unwilling states by force, economic pressure, or otherwise. The constitution of the League to provide, however, that decrees against an American Power shall be enforced by the nations of this hemisphere, and decrees against a country of the eastern hemisphere by the Powers of that hemisphere.

Article XIV provides for the establishment of a "permanent court of international justice," but its powers are limited to hearing and determining "any matter which the parties recognize as suitable for submission to it for arbitration" under Article XIII.

Team Work. With the plan agreed upon by the speakers, the brief made out, and the material distributed, each speaker can go to work in earnest to prepare his single speech. The best method has been outlined in this book. His notes should be accurate, clear, easily manipulated. His quotations should be exact, authoritative. By no means should he memorize his speech. Such stilted delivery would result in a series of formal declamations. With his mind stocked with exactly what his particular speech is to cover, yet familiar enough with the material of his colleagues to use it should he need it, the debater is ready for the contest.

Manipulating Material. The speakers on a side should keep all their material according to some system. If cards are used, arguments to be used in the main debate might be arranged in one place, material for rebuttal in another, quotations and statistics in still another. Then if the other side introduces a point not anticipated it should be easy to find the refuting or explaining material at once to counteract its influence in the next speech, if it should be disposed of at once. If slips of paper are used, different colors might indicate different kinds of material. Books, papers, reports, to be used should always be within available distance. While a speaker for the other side is advancing arguments the speaker who will follow him should be able to change, if necessary, his entire plan of defense or attack to meet the manœuver. He should select from the various divisions upon the table the material he needs, and launch at once into a speech which meets squarely all the contentions advanced by his predecessor. This instantaneous commandeering of material is likely to be most usual in rebuttal, but a good debater must be able to resort to it at a second's notice.

The First Affirmative Speaker. The first affirmative speaker must deliver some kind of introduction to the contentions which his side intends to advance. It is his duty to be concise and clear in this. He must not use too much time. If the proposition needs defining and applying he must not fail to do it. He must not give the negative the opportunity to explain and apply to its own purposes the meaning of the proposition. He should state in language which the hearers will remember exactly what the issues are. He can help his own side by outlining exactly what the affirmative intends to prove. He may indicate just what portions will be treated by his colleagues. He should never stop with merely introducing and outlining. Every speaker must advance proof, the first as well as the others. If the preliminary statements by the first affirmative speaker are clearly and convincingly delivered, and if he places a few strong, supporting reasons before the judges, he will have started his side very well upon its course of debating. The last sentences of his speech should drive home the points he has proved.

The First Negative Speaker. The first negative speaker either agrees with the definitions and application of the proposition as announced by the first affirmative speaker or he disagrees with them. If the latter, the mere statement of his disagreement is not sufficient. Contradiction is not proof. He must refute the definition and application of the proposition by strong reasoning and ample proof. If his side does not admit the issues as already presented he must explain or prove them away and establish in their place the issues his side sees in the discussion. When the two sides disagree concerning the issues there is a second proposition erected for discussion at once and the argument upon this second matter may crowd out the attempted argument upon the main proposition. To obviate such shifting many schools have the sides exchange briefs or statements of issues before the debate so that some agreement will be reached upon essentials.

In addition to the matters just enumerated the first negative speaker should outline the plan his side will follow, promising exactly what things will be established by his colleagues. If he feels that the first affirmative speaker has advanced proofs strong enough to require instant refutation he should be able to meet those points at once and dispose of them. If they do not require immediate answering, or if they may safely be left for later refutation in the regular rebuttal, he may content himself with simply announcing that they will be answered. He should not allow the audience to believe that his side cannot meet them.

He must not give the impression that he is evading them. If he has to admit their truth, let him frankly say so, showing, if possible, how they do not apply or do not prove all that is claimed for them, or that though they seem strong in support of the affirmative the negative side has still stronger arguments which by comparison refute at least their effect.

The first negative speaker should not stop with mere refutation. If the first affirmative has advanced proofs, and the first negative disposes of them, the debate is exactly where it was at the beginning. The negative speaker must add convincing arguments of his own. It is a good thing to start with one of the strongest negative arguments in the material.

The Second Affirmative and Second Negative Speakers. The second affirmative and the second negative speakers have very much the same kind of speech to make. Taking the immediate cues from the preceding speaker each may at first pay some attention to the remarks of his opponent. Here again there must be quickly decided the question already brought up by the first negative speech—shall arguments be refuted at once or reserved for such treatment in rebuttal? When this decision is made the next duty of each of these second speakers is to advance his side according to the plan laid down by his first colleague. He must make good the advance notice given of his team.

Each position of a debater has its peculiar tasks. The middle speaker must not allow the interest aroused by the first to lag. If anything, his material and manner must indicate a rise over the opening speech.

He must start at the place where the first speaker stopped and carry on the contention to the place at which it has been agreed he will deliver it to the concluding speaker for his side. If this connection among all the speeches of one side is quite plain to the audience an impression of unity and coherence will be made upon them. This will contribute to the effect of cogent reasoning. They will realize that instead of listening to a group of detached utterances they have been following a chain of reasoning every link of which is closely connected with all that precedes and follows.

The Concluding Affirmative Speaker. The concluding affirmative speaker must not devote his entire speech to a conclusion by giving an extensive summary or recapitulation. He must present arguments. Realizing that this is the last chance for original argument from his side he may be assigned the very strongest argument of all to deliver, for the effect of what he says must last beyond the concluding speech of the negative. It would likewise be a mistake for him to do nothing more than argue in his concluding speech. Several persons have intervened since his first colleague outlined their side and announced what they would prove. It is his duty to show that the affirmative has actually done what it set out to do. By amplifying and diminishing he may also show how the negative had not carried out its avowed intention of disproving the affirmative's position and proving conclusively its own. The concluding speech for the affirmative is an excellent test of a debater's ability to adapt himself to conditions which may have been entirely unforeseen when the debate began, of his keenness in analyzing the strength of the affirmative and exposing the weakness of the negative, of his power in impressing the arguments of his colleagues as well as his own upon the audience, and of his skill in bringing to a well-rounded, impressive conclusion his side's part in the debate.

The Concluding Negative Speaker. The concluding negative speaker must judge whether his immediate predecessor, the concluding affirmative speaker, has been able to gain the verdict of the judges. If he fears that he has, he must strive to argue that conviction away. He too must advance proof finally to strengthen the negative side. He must make his speech answer to his first colleague's announced scheme, or if some change in the line of development has been necessitated, he must make clear why the first was replaced by the one the debaters have followed. If the arguments of the negative have proved what it was declared they would, the last speaker should emphasize that fact beyond any question in any one's mind. Finally he should save time for a fitting conclusion. This brings the debate proper to a close.

Restrictions in Rebuttal. In rebuttal—if it be provided—the main restrictions are two. The speeches are shorter than the earlier ones. No new lines of argument may be introduced. Only lines of proof already brought forward may be considered. Since the speeches are shorter and the material is restricted there is always the disposition to use rebuttal speeches for refutation only. This is a mistake. Refute, but remember always that constructive argument is more likely to win decisions than destructive. Dispose of as many points of the opponents as possible, but reiterate the supporting reasons of your own. Many speakers waste their rebuttals by trying to cover too many points. They therefore have insufficient time to prove anything, so they fall back upon bare contradiction and assertion. Such presentations are mere jumbles of statements. Choose a few important phases of the opposing side's contention. Refute them. Choose the telling aspects of your own case. Emphasize them.

Manner in Debating. Be as earnest and convincing in your speeches as you can. Never yield to the temptation to indulge in personalities. Recall that other speakers should never be mentioned by name. They are identified by their order and their side, as "The first speaker on the affirmative" or "The speaker who preceded me," or "My colleague," or "My opponent." Avoid using these with tones and phrases of sarcasm and bitterness. Be fair and courteous in every way. Never indulge in such belittling expressions as "No one understands what he is trying to prove. He reels off a string of figures which mean nothing." Never indulge in cheap wit or attempts at satiric humor.

Prepare so adequately, analyze so keenly, argue so logically, speak so convincingly, that even when your side loses, your opponents will have to admit that you forced them to do better than they had any idea they could.

CHAPTER XIII

SPEAKING UPON SPECIAL OCCASIONS

Speech-making in the Professions. If a student enter a profession in which speech-making is the regular means of gaining his livelihood—as in law, religion, or lecturing—he will find it necessary to secure training in the technical methods applying to the particular kind of speech-making in which he will indulge. This book does not attempt to prepare any one for mastery of such special forms. The student will, however, be helping himself if he examines critically every delivery of a legal argument, sermon, or lecture he hears, for many of the rules illustrated by them and the impressions made by their speakers, can be transferred as models to be imitated or specimens to be avoided in his own more restricted and less important world.

Speaking upon Special Occasions. Every American may be called upon to speak upon some special occasion. If he does well at his first appearance he may be invited or required by circumstances to speak upon many occasions. The person who can interest audiences by effective delivery of suitable material fittingly adapted to the particular occasion is always in demand. Within the narrower confines of educational institutions the opportunities for the student to appear before his schoolmates are as numerous as in real life. Some preliminary knowledge coupled with much practice will produce deep satisfaction upon successful achievement and result in rapid steps of self-development.

Without pretending to provide for all possible circumstances in which students and others may be called upon to speak, this chapter will list some of the special occasions for which speeches should be prepared.

Speeches of Presiding Officers. On practically all occasions there is a presiding officer whose chief duty is to introduce to the audience the various speakers. The one great fault of speeches of introduction is that they are too long. The introducer sincerely means not to consume too much time, but in the endeavor to do justice to the occasion or the speaker he becomes involved in his remarks until they wander far from his definite purpose. He wearies the audience before the important speaker begins. An introducer should not become so unconscious of his real task as to fall into this error. In other cases the fault is not so innocent. Many a person called upon to introduce a speaker takes advantage of the chance to express his own opinions. He drops into the discourtesy of using for his own ends a condition of passive attention which was not created for him. One large audience which had assembled to hear a lecturer was kept from listening to him while for twenty minutes the introducer aired his own pet theories. Of course members of the audience discussed among themselves the inappropriateness of such remarks, but it is doubtful whether any criticism reached the offender.

A newspaper recently had the courage to voice the feelings of audiences.

> It seems that a good deal of the time of the audience at the Coliseum the other night was taken by those who introduced the speakers of the evening. We are told in one account of the meeting that the audience was at times impatient of these preliminaries and even howled once or twice for those it had come to hear.... We are informed that all those introducing the speakers said something about not having risen to speak at length, and that one of them protested his inability to speak with any facility. Both these professions are characteristic of those introducing speakers of the evening. Yet, strangely enough, the same always happens. That is, the preliminaries wear the audience out before the people it came to hear can get at it.

In introducing a speaker never be too long-winded. Tactfully, gracefully, courteously, put before the audience such facts as the occasion, the reason for the topic of the speech, the fitness and appropriateness of the choice of the speaker, then present the man or woman. Be extremely careful of facts and names. A nominating speaker at a great political convention ruined the effect of a speech by confusedly giving several first names to a distinguished man. It is embarrassing to a speaker to have to correct at the very beginning of his remarks a misstatement made by the presiding officer. But a man from one university cannot allow the audience to identify him with another. The author of a book wants its title correctly given. A public official desires to be associated in people's minds with the department he actually controls.

The main purpose of a speech of introduction is to do for the succeeding speaker what the chapter on beginning the speech suggested—to render the audience attentive and well-disposed, to introduce the topic, and in addition to present the speaker.

Choosing a Theme. The speaker at a special occasion must choose the theme with due regard to the subject and the occasion. Frequently his theme will be suggested to him, so that it will already bear a close relation to the occasion when he begins its preparation. The next matter he must consider with extreme care is the treatment. Shall it be serious, informative, argumentative, humorous, scoffing, ironic? To decide this he must weigh carefully the significance of the occasion. Selecting the inappropriate manner of treatment means risking the success of the speech. Recall how many men and speeches you have heard criticized as being "out of harmony with the meeting," or "not in spirit with the proceedings," and you will realize how necessary to the successful presentation is this delicate adjustment of the speech to the mood of the circumstances.

The After-dinner Speech. When men and women have met to partake of good food under charming surroundings and have enjoyed legitimate gastronomic delights it is regrettable that a disagreeable element should be added by a series of dull, long-winded, un-appropriate after-dinner speeches. The preceding adjectives suggest the chief faults of those persons who are repeatedly asked to speak upon such occasions. They so often miss the mark. Because after-dinner speaking is so informal it is proportionally difficult. When called upon, a person feels that he must acknowledge the compliment by saying something. This, however, is not really enough. He must choose his theme and style of treatment from the occasion. If the toastmaster assign the topic he is safe so far as that is concerned, but he must still be careful of his treatment.

A speaker at a dinner of the Phi Beta Kappa Society, in which membership is awarded for rank in cultural as contrasted with practical, technical studies, seized upon the chance to deliver a rather long, quite detailed legal explanation of the parole system for convicted offenders against laws. At a dinner given by the Pennsylvania Society in a state far from their original homes the members were praised to the skies for preserving the love of their native state and marking their identity in a district so distant and different. This was quite appropriate for an introduction but the speaker then turned abruptly to one of his political speeches and berated the foreigner in America for not becoming at once an entirely made-over citizen. The speech contradicted its own sentiments. A wrong emphasis was placed upon its material. A disquieting impression was made upon the Pennsylvanians. At the conclusion they felt that they were guilty for having kept the love of their native soil; according to the tone of the speaker they should have accepted their new residence and wiped out all traces of any early ties.

An after-dinner speaker should remember that dinners are usually marks of sociability, goodfellowship, congratulation, celebration, commemoration. Speeches should answer to such motives. The apt illustration, the clever twist, the really good story or anecdote, the surprise ending, all have their places here, if they are used with grace, good humor, and tact. This does not preclude elements of information and seriousness, but such matters should be introduced skilfully, discussed sparingly, enforced pointedly.

The Commemorative Speech. Besides dinners, other gatherings may require commemorative addresses. These speeches are longer, more formal. The success of a debating team, the successful season of an athletic organization, the termination of a civic project, the election of a candidate, the celebration of an historic event, the tribute to a great man, suggest the kinds of occasions in which commemorative addresses should be made.

Chosen with more care than the after-dinner speaker, the person on such an occasion has larger themes with which to deal, a longer time for their development, and an audience more surely attuned to sympathetic reception. He has more time for preparation also. In minor circumstances, such as the first three or four enumerated in the preceding paragraph, the note is usually congratulation for victory. Except in tone and length these speeches are not very different from after-dinner remarks. But when the occasion is more dignified, the circumstances more significant, addresses take on a different aspect. They become more soberly judicial, more temperately laudatory, more feelingly impressive. At such times public speaking approaches most closely to the old-fashioned idea of oratory, now so rapidly passing away, in its attempt to impress upon the audience the greatness of the occasion in which it is participating. The laying of a corner-stone, the completion of a monument or building, a national holiday, the birthday of a great man, the date of an epoch-marking event, bring forth eulogistic tributes like Webster's speech at Bunker Hill, Lincoln's Gettysburg Address, Secretary Lane's Flag Day speech.

False Eloquence. The beginner will not have many opportunities of delivering such remarkable addresses, but in his small sphere he will have chances to do similar things. He must beware of several faults of which the unwary are usually guilty. Recognizing the wonderful eloquence of the masterpieces of such kinds of address he may want to reproduce its effects by imitating its apparent methods. Nothing could be worse. The style of the great eulogy, born of the occasion and the speaker, becomes only exaggerated bombast and nonsense from the lips of a student. Exaggeration, high sounding terms, flowery language, involved constructions, do not produce eloquence in the speaker. They produce discomfort, often smiles of ridicule, in the audience. Many a student intending to cover himself with glory by eulogizing the martyred McKinley or the dead Roosevelt has succeeded only in covering himself with derision. Simplicity, straightforwardness, fair statement, should be the aims of beginning speakers upon such occasions.

Speeches of Presentation and Acceptance. Standing between the two classes of speeches just discussed are speeches of presentation and acceptance. In practically all circumstances where such remarks are suitable there are present mingled feelings of celebration and commemoration. There is joy over something accomplished, and remembrance of merit or success. So the person making a speech of presentation must mingle the two feelings as he and the audience experience them. Taking his cue from the tone of the occasion he must fit his remarks to that mood. He may be as bright and sparkling and as amusing as a refined court jester. He may be as impressive and serious as a judge. The treatment must be determined by the circumstances.

The speaker who replies must take his cue from the presenter. While the first has the advantage of carrying out his plan as prepared, the second can only dimly anticipate the theme he will express. At any rate he cannot so surely provide his beginning. That must come spontaneously from the turn given the material by his predecessor, although the recipient may pass by a transition to the remarks he prepared in advance.

The observations which obtain in the presentation and acceptance of a material object—as a book, a silver tea set, a medal, an art gallery—apply just as well to the bestowal and acceptance of an honor, such as a degree from a university, an office, an appointment as head of a committee or as foreign representative, or membership in a society. Speeches upon such occasions are likely to be more formal than those delivered upon the transfer of a gift. The bestower may cite the reasons for the honor, the fitness of the recipient, the mutual honors and obligations, and conclude with hopes of further attainments or services. The recipient may reply from a personal angle, explaining not only his appreciation, but his sense of obligation to a trust or duty, his methods of fulfilling his responsibilities, his modestly phrased hope or belief in his ultimate success.

The Inaugural Speech. In this last-named respect the speech of the recipient of an honor is closely related to the speech of a person inaugurated to office. This applies to all official positions to which persons are elected or appointed. The examples which will spring into students' minds are the inaugural speeches of Presidents of the United States. A study of these will furnish hints for the newly installed incumbent of more humble positions. In material they are likely to be retrospective and anticipatory. They trace past causes up to present effects, then pass on to discuss future plans and methods. Every officer in his official capacity has something to do. Newspaper articles will give you ideas of what officials should be doing. The office holder at the beginning of his term should make clear to his constituency, his organization, his class, his society, his school, just what he intends to try to do. He must be careful not to antagonize possible supporters by antagonistic remarks or opinions. He should try to show reason and expediency in all he urges. He should temper satisfaction and triumph with seriousness and resolve. Facts and arguments will be of more consequence than opinions and promises. The speech should be carefully planned in advance, clearly expressed, plainly delivered. Its statements should be weighed, as everyone of them may be used later as reasons for support or attack. To avoid such consequences the careful politician often indulges in glittering generalities which mean nothing. A student in such conditions should face issues squarely, and without stirring up unnecessary antagonism, announce his principles clearly and firmly. If he has changed his opinion upon any subject he may just as well state his position so that no misunderstanding may arise later.

In the exercise of his regular activities a person will have many opportunities to deliver this kind of speech.

The Nominating Speech. Recommendation of himself by a candidate for office does not fall within the plan of this book. Students, however, may indulge in canvassing votes for their favorite candidates, and this in some instances, leads to public speaking in class and mass meetings, assemblies, and the like. Of similar import is the nominating speech in which a member of a society, committee, meeting, offers the name of his candidate for the votes of as many as will indorse him. In nominating, it is a usual trick of arrangement to give first all the qualifications of the person whose election is to be urged, advancing all reasons possible for the choice, and uttering his name only in the very last words of the nominating speech. This plan works up to a cumulative effect which should deeply impress the hearers at the mention of the candidate's name.

In nominating speeches and in arguments supporting a candidate the deliverer should remember two things. Constructive proof is better than destructive attack; assertion of opinion and personal preference is not proof. If it seems necessary at times to show the fitness of one candidate by contrast with another, never descend to personalities, never inject a tone of personal attack, of cheap wit, of ill-natured abuse. If such practices are resorted to by others, answer or disregard them with the courteous attention they deserve, no more. Do not allow yourself to be drawn into any discussion remote from the main issue—the qualifications of your own candidate. If you speak frequently upon such a theme—as you may during an extended campaign—notice which of your arguments make the strongest impressions upon the hearers. Discard the weaker ones to place more and more emphasis upon the convincing reasons. Never fail to study other speakers engaged in similar attempts. American life every day provides you with illustrations to study.

The Speech in Support of a Measure. When, instead of a candidate, you are supporting some measure to be adopted, some reform to be instituted, some change to be inaugurated, your task is easier in one respect. There will be less temptation to indulge in personal matters. You will find it easier to adhere to your theme. In such attempts to mold public opinion—whether it be the collective opinion of a small school class, or a million voters—you will find opportunities for the inclusion of everything you know of the particular subject and of all human nature. Convinced yourself of the worthiness of your cause, bend every mental and intellectual effort to making others understand as you do, see as you do. If your reasoning is clear and converting, if your manner is direct and sincere, you should be able to induce others to believe as you do.

The Persuasive Speech. In public speaking upon occasions when votes are to be cast, where reforms are to be instituted, where changes are to be inaugurated, you have not finished when you have turned the mental attitude, and done no more. You must arouse the will to act. Votes must be cast for the measure you approve. The reform you urge must be financed at once. The change must be registered. To accomplish such a purpose you must do more than merely prove; you must persuade.

In the use of his power over people to induce them to noble, high-minded action lies the supreme importance of the public speaker.

EXERCISES

1. Choose some recent event which you and your friends might celebrate by a dinner. As toastmaster, deliver the first after-dinner remarks drawing attention to the occasion and introducing some one to speak.

2. Deliver the after-dinner speech just introduced.

3. Introduce some other member of the class, who is not closely connected with the event being celebrated, and who therefore is a guest.

4. Deliver this speech, being careful to make your remarks correspond to the preceding.

5. A debating team has won a victory. Deliver the speech such a victory deserves.

6. An athletic team has won a victory. As a non-participant, present the trophy.

7. An athletic team has finished a season without winning the championship. Speak upon such a result.

8. The city or state has finished some great project. Speak upon its significance.

9. Address an audience of girls or women upon their right to vote.

10. Speak in approval of some recently elected official in your community.

11. Choose some single event in the history of your immediate locality. Speak upon it.

12. Deliver a commemorative address suitable for the next holiday.

13. Bring into prominence some man or woman connected with the past of your community.

14. An unheralded hero.

15. "They also serve who only stand and wait."

16. "Peace hath her victories no less renowned than war."

17. Deliver the speech to accompany the presentation of a set of books.

18. Present to your community some needed memorial park, building, or other monument.

19. Accept the gift for the community.

20. Challenge another class to debate.

21. Urge upon some organization support of some civic measure.

22. As a representative of the students present some request to the authorities.

23. A meeting has been called to hear you because of your association with some organization or movement. Deliver the speech.

24. Some measure or movement is not being supported as it should be. A meeting of people likely to be interested has been called. Address the meeting.

25. Appeal to your immediate associates to support some charitable work.

26. Some organization has recently started a new project. Speak to it upon its task.

27. An organization has successfully accomplished a new project. Congratulate it.

28. Some early associate of yours has won recognition or success or fame away from home. He is about to return. Speak to your companions showing why they should honor him.

29. Choose some person or event worthy of commemoration. Arrange a series of detailed topics and distribute them among members of the class. Set a day for their presentation.

30. Choose a chairman. On the appointed day have him introduce the topic and the speakers.